Bill Jones encourages readers of his newest book to "better master the Word of God and . . . allow the Word of God to better master you." If that exhortation reflects the longing of your heart, then *Putting Together the Puzzle of the New Testament* will effectively help you to fulfill your desire. This book pulls together the twenty-seven books of the New Testament into one compelling story, powerfully motivating you to more diligently follow Christ.

JOSH D. MCDOWELL
Author, *Evidence That Demands a Verdict* and *More Than a Carpenter*

In another of his unique tools for individual or group Bible study, Bill Jones gives us a plan for New Testament study on the pattern of his earlier, widely used *Putting Together the Puzzle of the Old Testament.* He leads the reader in putting together a unified New Testament in a way that is simple to follow and easy to remember. His charts and maps make sure of that. But, at the same time, the text is profound in scholarship and vibrant in life-transforming application.

ROBERTSON MCQUILKIN
Author, *Understanding and Applying the Bible*

Too many Christians read their Bibles the way they might read a book of quotations. They find lots of good inspiring and memorable lines, but they don't experience the full power of God's miraculous book. This volume by Bill Jones is a powerful antidote to fragmented Bible reading.

DAVID NEFF
Editor-in-Chief, *Christianity Today*

For first-time readers, the New Testament may well appear as a puzzle. But put all the pieces together and a beautiful picture emerges—one that can change the way we look at everything. In this book, Dr. Bill Jones does exactly that. The breadth of his material not only shines light on the context of the story but also takes the reader into deeper levels of God's Word for growth and maturity.

DR. LEIGHTON FORD
President, *Leighton Ford Ministries*

Bill has a unique gift of seeing the big picture and making it understandable for all of us. This is absolutely one of the best resources out there for New Testament overview study.

DR. HANS FINZEL
President, WorldVenture
Author, *The Top Ten Mistakes Leaders Make*

Dr. Jones's ability to develop, compile, and share valuable information with all of his readers is exceptional. This document is a great source of quality content and relevant information. A must-read for everybody who is serious about studying the Bible.

DR. JEFFREY D. DE LEON
President, Latin American School of Theological Studies

I highly recommend this book for individuals, small groups, and even large classes who want to "work hard" and "have fun" gaining a clearer grasp of the entire New Testament. And this book will be most effective if studied in conjunction with Dr. Jones' equally excellent book, *Putting Together the Puzzle of the Old Testament*.

DR. GEORGE W. MURRAY
Chancellor, Columbia International University

This book is not only a learning tool for the Bible student but also a gathering of detail that yields insight and understanding as one seeks out the person of God. It provides not just more knowledge but will better enable the reader to take the message of Christ into the marketplace.

MARVIN R. SCHUSTER
Chairman of the Board, Schuster Enterprises, Inc.

Many Bible teachers can disassemble the text to facilitate analysis. The gift of insightful synthesis is rare. Most attempts at simplification end up in superficiality. Not so with Bill Jones. While making the New Testament accessible to learners on many levels, Bill relentlessly reminds us that the Great Commandment and the Great Commission frame the picture on the puzzle box.

DR. RALPH E. ENLOW JR.
Executive Director, Association for Biblical Higher Education

The reading of the Bible becomes to some people at best tiresome and at worst boring, simply because they only see pieces and not the whole picture. Dr. Jones has solved that problem by putting all the pieces together in a simple yet beautiful way, such that the reading of the Word of God becomes a great joy. It is clear, simple, and yet powerful.

RIGHT REVEREND ALEXIS BILINDABAGABO
Bishop of Gahini Diocese, Rwanda

Do you desire to better understand the Bible and to learn how it all fits together? Do you want to know how the Bible should personally affect your life? Then this book, along with Bill's book on the Old Testament, is perfect for you! Not only does Bill organize the material in a way that is easy to understand, it is also very easy to remember!

TOBIN CASSELS
President, Southeastern Freight Lines

For those who desire to love Jesus with all their hearts, God's Word leads them down that path. Today's Christians, young and old alike, desperately need to return to Scripture. Yet believers often seem overwhelmed at that thought. Once again, my friend Bill Jones brings clarity to the New Testament in a way that is compelling and easy to remember.

BARRY ST. CLAIR
Author and speaker

Bill Jones made the New Testament understandable so that any Sunday school teacher can teach the Bible clearly and accurately.

AARON MEYERS
Retired President, Tom James International

Bill Jones's book has helped lay people put together the puzzle of the New Testament in a very concise and simple way. If every layman could read this book, they could have a better grasp of the New Testament and become dedicated disciples of Jesus Christ.

ELMER L. TOWNS
Dean, School of Religion, Liberty University

Many people know bits and pieces of information concerning the New Testament but are unclear on the message of the New Testament as a whole. Bill Jones's work should prove useful in helping individuals and Bible study groups to make sense of where the pieces fit into the overall framework of the New Testament.

JOEL F. WILLIAMS
Co-editor, *Mission in the New Testament: An Evangelical Approach*

Bill Jones follows up on his outstanding earlier book, *Putting Together the Puzzle of the Old Testament*, with his new book, *Putting Together the Puzzle of the New Testament*. This will assist those who study the New Testament by helping them get a grasp on the teachings of the New Testament. A must-have book for Christians to have at hand for a thorough reference.

JOHN E. KYLE
President, Senior Leadership Exchange
Former Director, Mission to the World
Former Director, IVCF Missions and Urbana Conventions

Dr. Bill Jones has made another valuable contribution to students of the Bible, whether one is approaching God's Word as a scholar, a layman, or a new believer seeking to grasp the scope and meaning of the New Testament. *Putting Together the Puzzle of the New Testament* appropriately follows the author's parallel volume on the Old Testament. Asking the questions of what, where, when, why, and how, the charts and easy-to-understand outlines aid the reader in understanding the meaning of the text and the significance of the message. One of the most valuable insights is how the diverse testimonies of biblical writers focus on a unified purpose of God's glory in restoring all peoples to fellowship with Him.

JERRY RANKIN
President, International Mission Board, Southern Baptist Convention

PUTTING TOGETHER THE PUZZLE OF THE NEW TESTAMENT

BILL JONES

Authentic

COLORADO SPRINGS · MILTON KEYNES · HYDERABAD

Authentic Publishing
A Ministry of Biblica
We welcome your questions and comments.

USA	1820 Jet Stream Drive, Colorado Springs, CO 80921 www.authenticbooks.com
UK	9 Holdom Avenue, Bletchley, Milton Keynes, Bucks, MK1 1QR
	www.authenticmedia.co.uk
India	Logos Bhavan, Medchal Road, Jeedimetla Village, Secunderabad 500 055, A.P.

All Scripture quotations, unless otherwise indicated, are from the New American Standard Bible
(NASB). Copyright, The Lockman Foundation 1960, 1962, 1963, 1968, 1971, 1973, 1975, 1977,
1995.

Scripture marked TNIV taken from the Holy Bible, Today's New International Version® TNIV®
© Copyright 2001, 2005 by Biblica, Inc.™. Used by permission of Zondervan. All rights reserved
worldwide.

A catalog record for this book is available through the Library of Congress.

Editorial team: Bette Smyth, Dana Bromley, Dana Carrington
Cover and interior design: projectluz.com

Printed in the United States of America

For more information, write:
Crossover Communications International
P.O. Box 211755
Columbia, South Carolina 29221
803.691.0688
www.crossoverusa.org

DEDICATION

Though perhaps a small gesture, dedicating this book to the business-men of Columbia, South Carolina, truly represents the great appreciation I have for my friends who serve our Lord Jesus Christ in the workplace. Not only did they encourage me (*harass* comes closer to describing their methods at times) to start this project but they also allowed me to field test the material with them as the chapters developed.

One of God's greatest blessings in my life comes in the form of my "downtown" friends with whom I can get to know Christ more intimately and make Him known more passionately. May my marketplace friends freely allow the Word of God to master them as they diligently seek to master the Word of God.

I am truly grateful for their faithful support.

CONTENTS

PREFACE

For over two decades as I have taught in the seminary classroom of Columbia International University, a passion for making the Bible, God's Word, relevant and easy to understand has driven me. During this time, I have continually looked for better ways to teach the Bible so people can better understand it and be gripped by its message. While many people know *stories* from the Bible, they lack an understanding of the overall, unifying *story* of the Bible. Most Bible readers and students cannot put all the information together in a cohesive, chronological manner. This book, *Putting Together the Puzzle of the New Testament*, attempts to help correct that problem.

Its companion volume, *Putting Together the Puzzle of the Old Testament*, divided biblical history before the arrival of Jesus Christ into eight eras: *Nothing/Something, Exiting/Entering, United/Divided*, and *Scattered/Gathered*. This volume on the New Testament continues where the earlier volume left off, covering two more eras: *The Coming of Christ* and *The Going of the Church*. These two books have been arranged so that someone unfamiliar with the Bible can gain a quick and comprehensive overview of the Old and now the New Testaments, and those who have studied Scripture for years can receive much material that will take them deeper in their understanding.

I pray that this ministry tool will help you better master the Word of God and cause you to allow the Word of God to better master you. Let me know how it goes!

INTRODUCTION

How the New Testament Is Put Together

When it comes to knowing the Bible, we often possess more information about the New Testament than we do of the Old Testament. For example, more of us could probably come closer to naming the twelve disciples of Jesus found in the New Testament than identifying the twelve tribes of Israel found in the Old Testament. (By the way, if you have no clue as to either list or even the difference between the Old and New Testaments, don't worry. This book assumes you may not be as familiar with the Bible as you desire and exists to help you learn more about the New Testament section.)

But if we are not careful, we can make some big mistakes about the New Testament and not even realize it. Consider a common misunderstanding. Luke 4:13–14 says, "And when the devil had finished every temptation, he departed from Him [Jesus] until an opportune time. And Jesus returned to Galilee in the power of the Spirit; and news about Him spread through all the surrounding district." Based solely on these two verses, how much time elapses between the devil's departure and Jesus' return to Galilee? If you think that very little time elapses, you would not be alone, but you also would not be correct. The entire first year of Jesus' public ministry took place between these two verses! So, what happened during that year, and why did Luke not mention those events?

Other issues similar to this one make the New Testament seem a bit confusing. Yet they begin to make sense when we understand how the New Testament fits together.

To use the same analogy we used in the book *Putting Together the Puzzle of the Old Testament,* if we turned the New Testament into a giant thousand-piece puzzle, then this book provides you with the puzzle's box cover, giving the big picture of how all the pieces fit together. Additionally, this book identifies the corner and straight-edged pieces, providing a completed border of the puzzle. Having this framework in front of you allows you to more easily fill in the rest of the New Testament puzzle pieces.

Do you want to see how the various pieces of the New Testament fit together? Let's get started by examining the picture on the front of the puzzle box.

EXAMINING THE BOX COVER

If asked to paint a verbal picture of the contents of the New Testament, most people would give a description similar to the following: "The New Testament details how Jesus announces to the Jews the message of God's love and forgiveness. After His crucifixion and resurrection, He tells His followers to take this message to the Gentiles, or non-Jewish people groups."

Though not completely incorrect, this painting does not adequately describe the thrust of the New Testament. It makes it seem as though Jesus ministered only to the Jews during His earthly ministry. He didn't. The above statement also implies that Christ's concern for the Gentiles appeared almost as an afterthought, a last-minute idea before He ascended into heaven. Though the Lord did focus primarily on the Jews during His public ministry, we will see Him reaching out to the Gentiles as well.

If you have read the first book in this series, *Putting Together the Puzzle of the Old Testament*, you will remember that when properly assembled, the puzzle pieces of the Old Testament display a picture of **God receiving glory by restoring fellowship between all people groups and Himself through His Son, Jesus Christ**. If you didn't read that book, it may surprise you that the Old Testament refers to Jesus. Yet as you read the Old Testament, you discover it repeatedly prophesies the coming Messiah, or Christ, as the New Testament calls Him (see John 1:41). Not only that but we also see from the beginning of the Old Testament that God desires to reach all people groups with His message of love and forgiveness. God's heart has always longed for all the nations of the earth.

So what does the box cover of the New Testament puzzle look like? It looks exactly like the cover for the puzzle of the Old Testament. The whole thrust of the Bible, Old Testament and New Testament, communicates **God receiving glory by restoring fellowship between all people groups and Himself through His Son, Jesus Christ**.

With this in mind, let's open the box to the New Testament and begin putting together the pieces we find inside.

FINDING THE CORNER PIECES

To assemble any puzzle requires pouring out the contents of the box and organizing the pieces in some kind of order. This particular puzzle consists of twenty-seven pieces, or what we call the books of the New Testament. Let's arrange these pieces in the order we find them in our Bible's table of contents. Starting with Matthew and ending with Revelation results in the following list. Read down the columns rather than across the rows.

Matthew	Ephesians	Hebrews
Mark	Philippians	James
Luke	Colossians	1 Peter
John	1 Thessalonians	2 Peter
Acts	2 Thessalonians	1 John
Romans	1 Timothy	2 John
1 Corinthians	2 Timothy	3 John
2 Corinthians	Titus	Jude
Galatians	Philemon	Revelation

After sorting the pile of seemingly unrelated puzzle pieces, we next need to find the corner pieces. To discover the corners of the New Testament, you need a pen or pencil.

Using your pen, group the above puzzle pieces into three boxes. Trace a box around these books: Matthew, Mark, Luke, John, and Acts. Place the second set of books in what will seem like a very large box: Romans, 1 Corinthians, 2 Corinthians, Galatians, Ephesians, Philippians, Colossians, 1 Thessalonians, 2 Thessalonians, 1 Timothy, 2 Timothy, Titus, Philemon, Hebrews, James, 1 Peter, 2 Peter, 1 John, 2 John, 3 John, and Jude. One book remains, Revelation. Put this book in a box by itself. After practicing on the list above, it may benefit you for future reference to actually draw these boxes in the table of contents in your Bible.

	HISTORICAL BOOKS	EPISTOLARY BOOKS	PROPHETIC BOOKS
TITLES OF CATEGORY	Matthew to Acts	Romans to Jude	Revelation
NUMBER OF BOOKS IN CATEGORY	5 Books	21 Books	1 Book
EMPHASIS OF CATEGORY	Past	Present	Future

Each of the boxes you drew contains similar types of books, and they provide us with three (not four) corners around which to organize the twenty-seven puzzle pieces. The first box contains books that trace the history of Christ and His first followers. We know the first four of these (Matthew, Mark, Luke, and John) as the four Gospels. The word *gospel* comes from the old English word *godspell,* meaning either "God's story" or "good story," from which we get the phrase *good news.* The official title for each of these books begins with the phrase "The Gospel according to . . ." The full title of the fifth book is The Acts of the Apostles, which most people shorten to simply Acts. These five books provide the vast majority of the historical information of the New Testament.

The next box groups together all the books written to churches or the leaders of churches. We know these books as the Epistles, which means "letters," because their authors wrote them as such. Because this group contains a large number of puzzle pieces, or New Testament books, let's subdivide it even further.

Romans	1 Timothy	Hebrews
1 Corinthians	2 Timothy	James
2 Corinthians	Titus	1 Peter
Galatians	Philemon	2 Peter
Ephesians		1 John
Philippians		2 John
Colossians		3 John
1 Thessalonians		Jude
2 Thessalonians		

Draw one box around the books Romans, 1 and 2 Corinthians, Galatians, Ephesians, Philippians, Colossians, and 1 and 2 Thessalonians. Make another box around 1 and 2 Timothy, Titus, and Philemon. Draw a final box around the remaining books. If you drew the earlier boxes in your Bible, simply add two dotted lines in your table of contents: one between 2 Thessalonians and 1 Timothy, and the other between Philemon and Hebrews.

The first two smaller boxes contain books (letters) written by the apostle Paul. We separated them into two boxes because Paul wrote the first group of letters *to places*. For example, he wrote Romans to the church at Rome. Paul, however, addressed the other letters *to people,* not places: Timothy, Titus, and Philemon. The final group of epistles, called the General Epistles, stands out because each bears the author's name, with the exception of Hebrews (some people identify its author as the apostle Paul, but that is uncertain).

CATEGORY OF EPISTLES	PAUL'S LETTERS TO PLACES	PAUL'S LETTERS TO PEOPLE	GENERAL LETTERS FROM PEOPLE
TITLES OF EPISTLES	Romans to 2 Thessalonians	1 Timothy to Philemon	Hebrews to Jude
NUMBER OF EPISTLES	9 Books	4 Books	8 Books

Returning to the original boxes, we still have one remaining box, the box containing only one book. The official title is The Revelation to John. Notice the preposition states the revelation comes *to* John, not *from* John. Originally, God revealed the contents to John, who then passed it on to seven churches in the province of what people then called Asia, known to us today as part of Turkey. The book's focus on events that take place in the future makes this New Testament book unique.

With the corner pieces identified, we can now organize the New Testament books around the three corner pieces: Historical Books, Epistolary Books, and Prophetic Book.

27 Books of the New Testament

5 Historical Books	21 Epistolary Books	1 Prophetic Book
• Matthew	** *By Paul to Places*	• Revelation
• Mark	• Romans	
• Luke	• 1 Corinthians	
• John	• 2 Corinthians	
• Acts	• Galatians	
	• Ephesians	
	• Philippians	
	• Colossians	
	• 1 Thessalonians	

	• 2 Thessalonians
	** *By Paul to People*
	• 1 Timothy
	• 2 Timothy
	• Titus
	• Philemon
	** *By other Authors*
	• Hebrews
	• James
	• 1 Peter
	• 2 Peter
	• 1 John
	• 2 John
	• 3 John
	• Jude

Now that we've found the corners of the puzzle, we need to connect them by finding the straight-edged pieces that form the border of the puzzle's picture. Before doing so, however, let's take a moment to examine the frame that fits around the picture this New Testament puzzle ultimately produces.

THE FRAME SURROUNDING THE PUZZLE'S PICTURE

Appreciating the beauty of the New Testament requires an understanding of its context. We call this frame of reference the "Old Testament."

The Old Testament contains thirty-nine books. Thirteen of these books trace God's story from the beginning of the world to the years before the coming of Jesus Christ the Messiah. Let's look at the history, His-story, these books reveal.

Genesis portrays two major parts of the story. It begins by describing the creation of people and why their fellowship with God needs to be restored. Continuing the story, Genesis focuses on the beginning of the Hebrew nation, revealing that the Messiah would come from this nation and He would bless all the other nations.

Another major part of the story occurs in Exodus through Deuteronomy. These books explain how God delivers the Hebrews from captivity in Egypt. Once free from their captors, God gives them the Ten Commandments and instructs them on how He wants them to worship Him.

The books Joshua and Judges show the Hebrews entering Canaan, a land that God promised centuries earlier to give them. There they struggle with the tendency of turning away from the living God who loves and cares for them and turning to gods made by the hands of the Canaanites.

As time progresses, the Hebrews transition from a confederation of twelve loosely related tribes into a united kingdom ruled by three different kings. The books of 1 and 2 Samuel and part of 1 Kings tell what happens during this time period of Old Testament history.

Unfortunately, a rebellion takes place, splitting the kingdom into two countries, Israel and Judah. The end of 1 Kings and the beginning of 2 Kings chronicle these events—not the least of which involves Assyria conquering unfaithful Israel. Judah, however, does not remain free for long. The book of 2 Kings ends with Nebuchadnezzar conquering disobedient Judah and carrying the people into captivity in Babylon.

The books of Ezra and Nehemiah tell of God faithfully allowing the people of Judah to return to their Promised Land. There they wait for the coming Messiah, or Christ, until the beginning of the New Testament.

The following chart briefly summarizes these eight major "eras" of Old Testament history.

OLD TESTAMENT ERA	DESCRIPTION	SCRIPTURE
Nothing Era	God creates the human race out of nothing.	Genesis 1–11
Something Era	God turns the Hebrew race into something—a people of great size and significance.	Genesis 12–50
Exiting Era	The Hebrews exit Egypt but wander forty years in the wilderness because of their unbelief.	Exodus–Deuteronomy
Entering Era	The Hebrews enter the Promised Land and experience military victories and spiritual defeats.	Joshua–Judges
United Era	Three kings rule over the twelve Hebrew tribes in a united kingdom called Israel.	1 Samuel 1– 1 Kings 11
Divided Era	The kingdom divides into two nations: Israel and Judah. Assyria later conquers Israel.	1 Kings 12–2 Kings 23
Scattered Era	God scatters disobedient Judah by allowing Babylon to take Judah into captivity.	2 Kings 24–25
Gathered Era	God gathers Judah back to the Promised Land after seventy years of exile in Babylon.	Ezra–Nehemiah

Notice that the names of the eight eras divide into four pairs of opposite words: **Nothing/Something, Exiting/Entering, United/Divided, and Scattered/Gathered**.

Now turn in your Bible to where the Old and New Testaments meet. You'll find that Malachi wrote the last book found in the Old Testament, and Matthew wrote the first book found in the New Testament. Almost four centuries separate the events found in these two books. Students of the Bible call this time "the Silent Years" because no prophet speaks for God during this time. Yet the events that occur during these final years of the Gathered Era play an extremely important role. They help create the perfect timing for God to send the Messiah, Jesus Christ, in order to restore fellowship between Himself and all the people groups of the world. Taking a look at the events of the Gathered Era's Silent Years completes our frame of reference.

Four main groups rule the Jewish people during the years between the books of Malachi and Matthew. After conquering Babylon in 539 BC, Persia rules over the Promised Land until Alexander the Great defeats the Persians in 331 BC. After Alexander's death in 323 BC, four of his generals divide the territory into four smaller empires. One general named Ptolemy takes Egypt and the Promised Land, which by this time has taken the name Palestine. Another general, Seleucus, takes Syria and Babylon. For over a hundred years the Ptolemies treat the Jews favorably.

When the Seleucids conquer Palestine in 198 BC, favorable treatment of the Jews ends. The Seleucids aggressively seek to replace the Jewish culture with their own Greek culture. They severely punish anyone who worships on the Sabbath, practices circumcision, or observes any of the religious feasts. These new Greek rulers also seek to destroy the Hebrew Scriptures, which we call the Old Testament. They equate the God of the Bible with the Greek deity Jupiter, whose image they erected in the Jewish temple. The ultimate insult comes when the Seleucids desecrate the temple by sacrificing pigs, considered unclean animals, on its altar.

Eventually, the Jews rebel against their Greek masters and gain independence. These revolutionaries become known as the Maccabees because one of their leaders is called Judas the Maccabee, which means, "hammer." Freedom lasts from 167 to 63 BC, at which time the Roman general Pompey, a contemporary of Julius Caesar, conquers Palestine, bringing the Jews under the rule of the Romans.

The last three rulers make significant contributions in preparing for the coming of Christ, referred to as "the fullness of the time" in Galatians 4:4.

RULERS DURING THE SILENT YEARS

Persia	Greece	Israel	Rome

As a result of Alexander's conquests, the Greek language becomes almost universal. Wherever the Jews went, they spread their belief in one God, a thought attractive for many as people realized the inadequacies of paganism. Additionally, the Roman Empire establishes a vast network of roads and such a long-term peace that it becomes known as the Pax Romana.

CONTRIBUTIONS DURING THE SILENT YEARS

Greek language	Jewish monotheism	Roman roads and peace

Why do we consider these contributions important to the timing of the Messiah's coming? Because at that particular point in history, Christians could easily *travel* to the limits of their known world and *communicate* the message of God's love and forgiveness found in a personal relationship with God's Son, Jesus Christ. This overall perspective helps us to better appreciate the beauty of the resulting picture. Now let's return to assembling the puzzle of the New Testament.

LOOKING FOR STRAIGHT-EDGED PIECES

Assembling the straight-edged pieces produces the border of the puzzle. To find the straight-edged pieces for the New Testament, we need to look primarily in the historical category of books.

The first four books from the historical category, the Gospels, detail the life of Jesus Christ from His birth to the point when He ascends into heaven. Interestingly, one-third of the eighty-nine chapters in these books focus on the last few days of Christ's life out of approximately thirty-three years He lived on earth. We identify the time covered by the Gospels as the "Coming of Christ Era." We can shorten this title to the **Coming Era**.

The next major section of New Testament history deals with the followers of Christ going everywhere to proclaim that God loves the world so much that He sent the prophesied Messiah and that whoever believes in Him would not perish but have eternal life. The entire book of Acts, the fifth book found in the historical corner, relates to this mission, as do the epistolary books and the book of Revelation. We name this part of the New Testament the "Going of the Church Era," or simply the **Going Era**.

Putting together the Old Testament and the New Testament historical eras gives us ten units of time. Keep in mind that the Gathered Era includes the Silent Years.

ERAS OF OLD TESTAMENT	Nothing	Something	Exiting	Entering
	United	Divided	Scattered	Gathered
ERAS OF NEW TESTAMENT	Coming		Going	

Putting Together the Puzzle of the New Testament looks in much more detail at the Coming and Going historical eras of the New Testament. To accomplish our purpose, we will subdivide these two eras into smaller units of time called "periods."

We will divide the Coming Era into four time periods. The first period addresses the early years of Christ. During this time Christ gets little attention as He prepares for His important work. We call these years **Christ's Private Period**. The next clear unit of time in the life of Christ speaks of His three years of ministry to His disciples and the multitudes.

We label these three years **Christ's Public Period**. Numerous events occur during the last week of His life, many of them tragic. Because of all the suffering, we call these seven days **Christ's Trials Period**. Two days after His death, Christ rises victoriously from the grave, conquering the power of sin and death. For forty days He walks on earth with His followers before ascending into heaven. This final episode in the life of Christ we will name **Christ's Triumphant Period**. We can visualize the relationship between these four periods of time and the Coming of Christ Era by looking at the following diagram.

The Going of the Church Era also divides into four smaller units of time. The book of Acts begins with Christ ascending into heaven and His followers withdrawing to pray and to wait for the power that Christ had promised them. Because the followers of Christ spend much of this time by themselves in an upstairs room of a friend's house, we will call this time period the **Church's Private Period**. Ten days later, this power in the form of the Holy Spirit arrives and gives birth to what we know as the

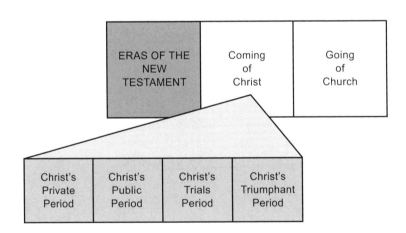

Church. Upon the arrival of the Holy Spirit the disciples immediately take the message of God's love and forgiveness to the masses. This begins the **Church's Public Period**. Throughout the last 25 percent of the book of

Acts, Paul endures imprisonment in one form or another. Though briefly freed sometime after the book of Acts closes, in 2 Timothy we find Paul once again in prison, awaiting execution. We know this unit of time as the **Church's Trials Period**. The book of Revelation discloses the ultimate destiny of the Church and what a glorious future it will be! The Church victoriously overcomes sin, death, and the devil through faith in Christ. Representatives from every people group spend eternity worshiping the Lord Jesus Christ. We call this period the **Church's Triumphant Period**.

Adding these four time periods associated with the Going of the Church Era to the four time periods associated with the Coming of Christ Era produces the following chart.

Now that we possess a general understanding of how the puzzle fits together, let's take a closer look at each of the eight historical periods of the New Testament. We will do this in a way that allows us to recall and communicate the New Testament story of God restoring fellowship between Himself and the nations through His Son, Jesus Christ.

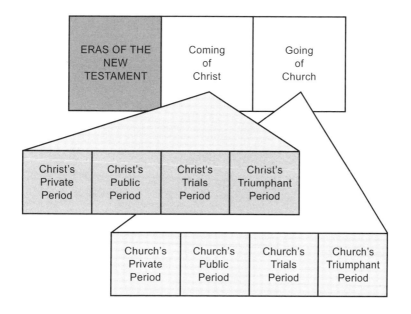

FOR NEXT TIME

You may be working through this material with a group. If so, choose one of the following options in preparing for next week's lesson, depending on the amount of time you can devote this week. This preparation time is intended to encourage you to seek to know God better through His Word.

If you are having an extremely busy week:	If you have a little extra time:	If you can't get enough:
read Matthew 1:1–4:11.	add Luke 1:1–4:13.	add John 1:1–18.

PERIOD #1

PERIOD #1

Christ's Private Period

We learned in the Introduction that we can easily group the twenty-seven books of the New Testament into three corners, or different categories. See if you can name them below, noting the number of books each category contains.

Category   Number of Books

1. _____   _____

2. _____   _____

3. _____   _____

The first and third of these categories provide us with a timeline from the birth of Christ to the end of time as we know it. We divided this timeline into two eras. To help us remember these two eras we gave them opposite names. Place these names in the chart below.

In order to more easily master the content of the New Testament, we divided the two eras into eight periods of time. Add the names of these eight time periods to the chart above. If your memory fails you, please look at the Introduction.

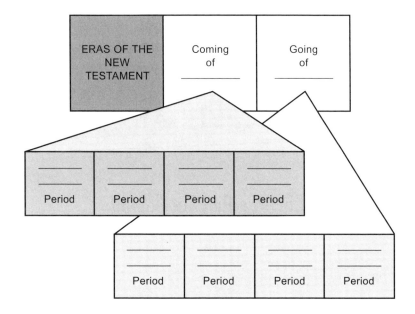

The next eight chapters, beginning with this chapter, take an in-depth look at these eight New Testament time periods. We will investigate each period by answering six important questions: What? How? Where? When? Why? and Who? Let's dig into the first time period of the New Testament, which covers the Private Period of Jesus Christ.

WHAT?

Adam and Eve's disobedience to the divine command not to eat of the tree of the knowledge of good and evil in the garden of Eden results in disaster. Terrible consequences immediately occur—broken fellowship with God proving the greatest of them all. Before expelling them from His presence, the God of hope promises (Genesis 3:15) to send them someone who will ultimately deliver the human race from sin and the power of evil.

Later God declares that this Savior, the Messiah, will come *for* the human race *through* the Hebrew race. In Genesis 22:18 God promises that He will bless Abraham *so that* he and his offspring will be a blessing to all the nations of the earth (Galatians 3:8). Yet the people of God quickly forget the "so that." They focus solely on the fact that God has blessed them, and they ignore the fact that God desires the worship of all nations, the human race, not just the adoration of one specific people group.

God, however, relentlessly reminds His people throughout the Old Testament that He will send the promised Deliverer to the Hebrews and, through them, to the Gentiles. For thousands of years the people wait on God's perfect timing.

Finally, the moment arrives. God sends the Messiah, whom we know as Jesus Christ, in the form of a baby. For most of his life Jesus grows and develops in relative obscurity. This Private Period focuses on **the preparation of the Messiah,** as the Lord Jesus readies Himself for the task that God sent Him to accomplish.

The Private Period of Christ lasts for approximately thirty years, the longest-lasting period of the Coming of Christ Era. As you see in the chart below, however, the four writers of the Gospels devote very little of their books to this time period in the life of Christ.

CHRIST'S PRIVATE PERIOD

Matthew	Mark	Luke	John
3 ½ chapters	½ chapter	3 ½ chapters	½ chapter
(1:1–4:11)	(1:1–13)	(1:1–4:13)	(1:1–18)

People tend to think that by reading either Matthew or Luke they can get the whole story of this time in the life of Christ, but that is not the case. Each writer adds important information not mentioned by the others. Their combined versions give a fuller understanding of all that occurs during the Private Period of Christ. By harmonizing these two accounts we discover seven key items that tell the story of how God specifically prepares the Lord for His future ministry.

HOW?

The Private Period of Christ revolves around **seven groups of people**. Remembering these seven groups of people allows you to recount all the important events that occur during this New Testament time period. Though we find some of these people in the Gospel of Matthew and others in the Gospel of Luke, we can weave the seven groups together into one seamless tapestry.

The story begins in the city of Nazareth with God sending news to a young virgin named **Mary** that He will miraculously place His child in her womb. Despite the news of the pregnancy of his fiancée, **Joseph** righteously keeps her a virgin until after she delivers the promised Messiah. The baby arrives while Mary and Joseph register in Bethlehem for a census commanded by the Roman Caesar Augustus.

Popular tradition holds that the young couple stays in what we would consider a motel, because Luke 2:7 says, "There was no room for them in the inn." Yet, in every other place in Scripture, scholars translate the word used for *inn* in this passage as *guest room* (see Mark 14:14; Luke 22:11). This suggests that Mary and Joseph may have stayed in the crowded home of a relative. This option makes a lot of sense for several reasons. Financially, as we shall see in a moment, Mary and Joseph probably could not afford to stay long in an inn. Culturally, in those days people stayed with their relatives when possible. Architecturally, homes of that time had the stables attached to the house, not separated from it. Placing the expectant mother in the stable would allow her privacy and enable the other women to care for her. It would also provide more space in the guest room (inn) for the other relatives to come and go. Regardless, the required registration fills the town with crowds of people, limiting Mary and Joseph's options for housing. The circumstances force them to take refuge in a stable, which becomes the divine delivery room.

Interestingly, during this time of history the Jews raised many of their sacrificial lambs in the small city of Bethlehem. On the night of Jesus' birth, an angel announces to nearby **shepherds**, tending some of these future sacrificial lambs, the joyous good news that a Savior, Christ the Lord, had been born earlier that day. The shepherds hastily make their way to the city in order to worship the Messiah. Upon arriving (probably locating the family by asking where they might find a newborn baby), the shepherds discover Mary tending the ultimate Sacrificial Lamb, just as the angel said they would, lying in a manger, a box from which animals ate their food.

About six weeks later, Mary and Joseph travel the five or six miles from Bethlehem to the temple in Jerusalem in order to fulfill two obligations. Exodus 13:2 required parents to present their first-born child to the Lord (Luke 2:22–23). They also needed to obey a law found in Leviticus 12:1–8, requiring women to make an offering after the birth of a child. That Mary and Joseph offered two doves or pigeons (Luke 2:24), rather than a bird and a lamb, demonstrates their poverty, as seen in Leviticus 12:8. While at the temple, a godly man named **Simeon** takes the baby Jesus into his arms and proclaims that God has prepared this Child for the salvation of Jews and Gentiles. As Mary and Joseph stand listening in amazement to Simeon's words, an elderly woman, **Anna**, who prays in the temple night and day, comes to them. Upon seeing the Child, she begins thanking God and telling everyone that Jesus had come to free His people.

SEVEN GROUPS OF PEOPLE

	MATTHEW	LUKE
Born to Mary and Joseph	1:1–25	1:1–2:7
Worshiped by the shepherds		2:8–21
Honored by Simeon and Anna		2:22–40
Sought by the magi and Herod	2:1–23	
Taught by temple teachers		2:41–52
Baptized by John the Baptist	3:1–17	3:1–38
Tempted by the devil	4:1–11	4:1–13

After performing their required duties at the temple, Mary and Joseph return to Nazareth with Jesus (Luke 2:39). Sometime during the next two years (Matthew 2:16), Mary and Joseph receive an unexpected visit from some **magi**, or scholars who studied medicine, natural science, and the stars. As wise men, they probably knew of certain Old Testament prophecies, such as "a star shall come forth from Jacob, and a scepter shall rise from Israel" (Numbers 24:17). The magi—noticing an unusual occurrence, such as a comet or the conjunction of planets in the part of the sky they believed controls the destiny of the Jews—decide to pay a state visit to honor the birth of this new king.

Scripture does not mention the exact number of these wise men, though Christmas cards typically show three of them because they offered three types of gifts: gold, frankincense, and myrrh. Nor does Scripture tell us exactly from where they came. We do know, however, that they arrived from the east. They probably originated either from Persia—because magi had functioned there as philosophers and priests since the time of the prophet Daniel—or from Babylon, the birthplace of astrology.

They logically stop first in the capital city of Jerusalem, seeking to find the newborn king. The current Jewish ruler, **King Herod**, interrogates the chief priests and scribes to ascertain the prophesied birthplace of the Messiah (Matthew 2:4–6) as well as to discover the age of his potential rival (Matthew 2:7, 16). Herod deceitfully sends the magi to Bethlehem to locate the future ruler under the pretense of wanting to worship Jesus, though in reality he plans to murder Him. The wise men, however, follow the star to Nazareth (remember Luke 2:39), where they find Mary and Joseph living in a house (Matthew 2:11), caring not for baby Jesus (Luke 2:12), but for the now young child Jesus (Matthew 2:11). At that time in history, when you met a person of much greater rank, you would fall on your knees, touch your forehead to the ground or even prostrate yourself, and throw kisses in the direction of the superior. When the magi find the Lord Jesus, they fall down and worship Him.

God uses two dreams at this point to protect young Jesus from the jealous Herod. In the first dream God directs the magi to return home without reporting to Herod, thus keeping the exact location of the Child a secret. This protects Jesus from Herod who, now in a rampage, slaughters all the male children two years old and younger living in and around Bethlehem. This king's rage knows no bounds—he had already put to death a wife, three sons, and various in-laws to eliminate any perceived threat to his throne.

In the second dream God warns Joseph to flee with his family to Egypt until further notice. The gifts offered by the magi probably finance the expense of the journey. Moving the family to another country further protects the Lord Jesus from Herod's insanity, because the vast expanse of Egypt lies outside his jurisdiction.

Upon Herod's death, God uses two more dreams to recall Joseph and his family out of Egypt and to send them once again to Nazareth (Matthew 2:19–23), where Jesus grows in strength and wisdom (Luke 2:40). Scripture mentions only one specific incident during his growing-up years. At the age of twelve, Jesus travels with his earthly parents and many others to Jerusalem to celebrate the Passover Feast. At the end of the festivities, Mary and Joseph join the caravan to begin the return journey home, assuming Jesus was traveling with one of their relatives or friends in the group. That evening they realize Jesus' absence. It takes an entire day to backtrack to the city to look for Him. (It doesn't take much effort to imagine how they must have felt, wondering if they had lost the future Savior of the world!) On the third day, they finally find Jesus in the temple listening to the **teachers**, rabbis who explained the Old Testament.

The next time the Bible mentions Jesus almost twenty years have passed. All we know about the intervening years comes from Luke 2:52, which tells us that Jesus "kept increasing in wisdom and stature, and in favor with God and men."

The sixth key episode in the preparation of the Messiah concerns His baptism by **John the Baptist**, a relative of Jesus who lived in the mountains between Jerusalem and the Dead Sea. Though a peculiar man, John preaches a powerful message of repentance, baptizing people as they confess their disobedience to God. One day Jesus arrives from Galilee, wanting John to baptize Him. Since John the Baptist knows that his ministry serves only to prepare people for the coming ministry of Jesus (Luke 1:76–77; Matthew 1:21), he reluctantly obeys, baptizing Jesus in the Jordan River and thus identifying the sinless Savior with sinful humanity. After His baptism, Jesus begins to pray (Luke 3:21). As He does so, the Spirit of God descends on Him in the form of a dove, and a voice from heaven announces, "This is My beloved Son, in whom I am well-pleased."

After His baptism, Jesus departs immediately (Mark 1:12) for the wilderness, where He fasts for forty days and nights. This experience proves critical to the preparation of the Messiah, because during this time of solitude He, as a man, overcomes the devil's temptations (Matthew 4:2), meaning He does not rely on His divine powers. His human obedience in the face of temptation qualifies Him to serve as the payment for the penalty of all humanity's disobedience (Hebrews 2:17).

The **devil** tempts Jesus during the entire forty days and nights (Mark 1:13; Luke 4:2; Hebrews 4:15), though Scripture mentions only three specific instances. In the first temptation (Matthew 4:3–4), the devil uses Jesus' extreme hunger to entice Him to turn some of the many stones found scattered in the wilderness into bread. Jesus responds by quoting Deuteronomy 8:3.

During the second encounter (Matthew 4:5–7), the tempter takes the Lord to the highest part of the temple and, from this breath-taking position, tries to convince Jesus to jump. The devil buttresses his argument by reciting Psalm 91:11–12. He rationalizes that if Jesus truly is the Son of God, then nothing will happen to Him because God had promised that angels would guard Him by bearing Him up in their hands so that He would not strike His foot against a stone. This argument might trap someone unfamiliar with the scope of Scripture but not Jesus. He knew that God's promised protection did not give permission to intentionally create danger. He responds by quoting Deuteronomy 6:16.

The final recorded temptation shows the devil taking Jesus to a high mountain and showing Him all the kingdoms of the world. For this temptation to make sense, let's recall the theme of Scripture. The box cover of our puzzle displays a picture of God receiving glory by restoring fellowship between Himself and the nations through His Son, Jesus Christ. Later we will find that God accomplishes His purpose by crucifying Jesus as payment for mankind's disobedience. Here, however, the devil offers a shortcut. If the Son of God would simply fall down and worship him (remember the magi?), then the devil would give Jesus the nations—without Him having to endure the agony of the cross. Again Jesus quotes from Deuteronomy (6:13) saying, "You shall worship the Lord your God and serve Him only."

After the last recorded temptation, the devil leaves and angels come to care for the Lord Jesus. Luke adds, however, that the devil *temporarily* retreats only to wait for a more strategic time (Luke 4:13). This may refer to the night before Christ's crucifixion when Jesus struggles in fervent prayer over the prospect of the next day's ordeal. There in the garden of Gethsemane God also sends an angel to strengthen Jesus (Luke 22:43). Yet for now, Jesus successfully overcomes the devil, using Scripture that God gave to the Hebrews at the end of their wilderness experience. This Private Period has fully prepared Him for the next stage of His life, what we will call in the following chapter the Public Period of Christ.

At this point, we know what God did during this Private Period and how He went about it. Now let's look at where each of these events took place.

WHERE?

Scripture locates, fairly specifically, the events related to the seven groups of people identified with the Private Period of the Messiah. Let's begin with Mary and Joseph's journey to register for the census decreed by Caesar Augustus.

Their trip originates from Nazareth (1), a city on the side of a steep hill fourteen miles southwest of the Sea of Galilee and only a couple of miles from a main Roman road. Because the census required every male to register in the city of his ancestors, Joseph returns to Bethlehem (2) to record his name, occupation, property, and family.

It surprises some that Joseph would take Mary with him because of her condition and because he had not yet married her. It makes much more sense when we understand that engagements in that culture carried many of the legal rights of marriage, though forbidding sexual relations. Perhaps the greatest motivation involves their knowledge of the prophecy found in Micah 5:2, predicting Bethlehem as the place of the Messiah's birth.

SEVEN GROUPS OF PEOPLE

	MATTHEW	LUKE	WHERE
Born to Mary and Joseph	1:1–25	1:1–2:7	Bethlehem
Worshiped by the shepherds		2:8–2:21	Bethlehem
Honored by Simeon and Anna		2:22–40	Temple in Jerusalem
Sought by the magi and Herod	2:1–23		Bethlehem, Nazareth, and Egypt
Taught by temple teachers		2:41–52	Temple in Jerusalem
Baptized by John the Baptist	3:1–17	3:1–38	Jordan River
Tempted by the devil	4:1–11	4:1–13	Wilderness and temple

Sometime after arriving in Bethlehem, Mary gives birth to Jesus. As we learned above, the shepherds visit that night and honor the newborn Messiah. Eight days later Mary and Joseph give Him the name Jesus (Luke 2:21) and have Him circumcised.

A few weeks later, Mary and Joseph travel to Jerusalem (3) to present their first-born child (Luke 2:22; Exodus 13:2, 12) to the Lord and for Mary to offer her sacrifice (Luke 2:24; Leviticus 12:1–8). Upon entering the temple to fulfill these two obligations (Luke 2:27–28), Simeon and Anna honor Jesus.

Disagreement exists as to where the couple goes next. Many believe that Mary and Joseph return to Bethlehem because Herod sends the magi there (Matthew 2:8) to search for the Child. But Matthew's account never says the magi go to Bethlehem. It does say that they follow the star until it stands over the house of the Child (Matthew 2:9–11). Luke, on the other hand, clearly states that Mary and Joseph, after completing both of their lawful duties in the Jerusalem temple (Luke 2:39), return with Jesus to their own city of Nazareth.

Because Herod wanted to kill all children two years old and younger (Matthew 2:16), we suspect that sometime between the second and twenty-fourth month after the birth of the Messiah, Mary and Joseph took Jesus to Egypt (4) to protect Him from Herod's wrath.

Christ's Private Period

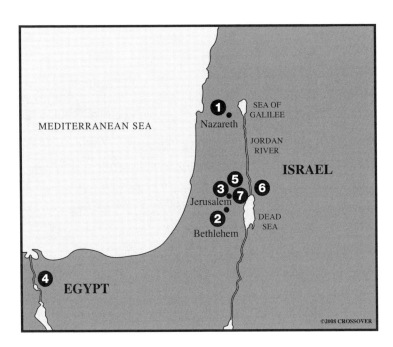

After Herod dies and danger to Jesus no longer exists, Mary and Joseph return to the land of Israel, or Palestine, as the Romans called it. God sends them back to the district of Galilee to live once again in their home city of Nazareth, where Jesus grows to an adult. Except for Jesus' trip to Jerusalem at the age of twelve when He interacted with the rabbis of the temple (5), we have no scriptural record of Jesus' life during this time. We can, however, assume that He visited Jerusalem during the three major annual feasts (the Feast of Unleavened Bread that occurs at Passover, the Feast of Weeks also called Pentecost, and the Feast of Booths or Tabernacles), as required by Scripture of every Jewish male (Deuteronomy 16:16).

The next major event during the Private Period of Christ finds the Messiah seeking John the Baptist to baptize Him in the Jordan River, which runs from the Sea of Galilee in the north of Palestine to the Dead Sea in the south, about sixty-five miles if drawn in a straight line. John baptizes Jesus in the Jordan River (6) somewhere between Jericho and the city of Bethany, or as Scripture calls it, "Bethany beyond the Jordan" (John 1:28), to differentiate it from the Bethany located two miles from Jerusalem.

The Spirit of God leads Jesus immediately after His baptism into the wilderness (7), where the devil tempts Him for forty days and nights. Other than when the tempter takes Jesus to the temple in Jerusalem, enticing Him to leap into the valley below without hurting Himself, Jesus spends the entire time in the Judean wilderness. Tradition locates the high mountain mentioned in Matthew 4:8 to be southwest of the city of Jericho.

Tracing the movement of Mary, Joseph, and Jesus shows that they traverse Palestine from the north to the south several times as well as take the trip to Egypt to avoid Herod's killing spree. Yet if we must mark a primary geographical point during the Private Period of Christ, we choose **Nazareth** because the Lord spends decades living and growing up in that city.

WHEN?

The Private Period of Christ does not occur in a vacuum. Notice some of the historical markers scattered about by our Gospel writers. The events of Christ's birth take place in the days of Herod the king (Matthew 2:1), when a decree goes out from Caesar Augustus, while Quirinius serves as governor of Syria (Luke 2:1–2). Christ's baptism and temptation occur during the fifteenth year of the reign of Caesar Tiberius when Pontius Pilate governs Judea as procurator, Herod Antipas governs Galilee as tetrarch, and his brother Philip governs the region of Ituraea and Trachonitis also as tetrarch. During this time Annas and Caiaphas sit as former and current high priest, respectively (Luke 3:1–2).

The above names, titles, and places provide the historical context of the life of Jesus by identifying the governing officials on three different levels. Caesars Augustus and Tiberius consecutively ruled the Roman Empire on the *imperial level* from 31 BC to AD 37. Their empire consisted of various nations or people groups such as the Jews, whom Rome had conquered. Over these various *regional levels* they appointed rulers possessing different levels of authority. In 40 BC, the Roman senate appointed Herod the Great as king over Palestine. By 37 BC, he officially consolidated his power and ruled until 4 BC. At Herod's death, Rome divided the governing of Palestine into three smaller regions. At the end of the Private Period of Christ, two of Herod's sons, Herod Antipas and Philip, ruled as tetrarchs over two of the regions. A Roman procurator, the infamous Pontius Pilate, oversaw the third region of Judea and Samaria from AD 26 to AD 36.

In addition to these political leaders, the Jewish people also had leaders on the *religious level* in the form of the high priest. Unfortunately, during this time the high priest served at the pleasure of Rome and focused more on the political situation than the religious one. The above passage from Luke mentions two of these high priests, Annas and his son-in-law

Caiaphas (John 18:13). Caiaphas ruled from AD 18 to AD 36. Knowing when each of these potentates ruled allows us to locate a fairly specific time frame for the seven key items found during the Private Period of Christ.

So when did the events of the Private Period of Christ occur? We can ascertain approximate dates for both the beginning and ending of this New Testament period by using clues from the Roman emperors, the Jewish king, and the Gospel writers.

Let's first examine when this period begins. The Roman Emperor Caesar Augustus decrees (Luke 2:1–2) the taking of a census, which occurs under Quirinius. Most historians place the Palestinian portion of this census between 6 and 4 BC, meaning the birth of Christ occurred *no earlier* than 6 BC. Because multiple historical records document the year of Herod the Great's death (Matthew 2:19) as 4 BC, we know that the birth of Jesus cannot occur *any later* than that date, which is at least four years earlier than the date traditionally set by our Gregorian calendar that separates BC (Before Christ) and AD (Anno Domini, Year of our Lord). As a result of these two historical boundaries, we can safely place the Messiah's arrival somewhere between 6 and 4 BC, which agrees with the clue in Matthew's gospel (Matthew 2:16) stating that Herod killed all the male children two years old and younger.

Well, what about the end of this period? The date of the fifteenth year of the reign of Roman Emperor Tiberius (Luke 3:1) determines when the baptism and temptation of Christ occur. Tiberius co-reigned with his father, Augustus, before his father died, thus providing two possible dates Luke could have used to mark the beginning of Tiberius' reign. If he uses the year when Tiberius begins to co-rule, then the baptism and temptation occur between AD 26 and AD 27. If he uses the year Augustus dies, then the baptism and temptation occurs between AD 28 and AD 29. A clue provided by John about Herod the Great allows us to choose the former of these two options. Not long after this period ends, the Jews tell Jesus (John 2:20) that it had taken forty-six years at that point to remodel the temple. If we add forty-six years to 20–19 BC, the approximate date Herod begins construction of the temple, then we arrive at a date of AD 26–27. Again, this date fits with the clue in Luke's gospel (Luke 3:23), which approximates the age of Jesus at about thirty years old when He begins His ministry. A 6 BC birth date makes Jesus about thirty-one to thirty-three years old, and a 4 BC birth date makes Him about twenty-nine to thirty-one years old. The range depends on whether Mary gave birth earlier or later in the year, January as compared to December, which would add or subtract an entire twelve months.

EVIDENCE	BEGINNING DATE	ENDING DATE
ROMAN EMPEROR	Caesar Augustus' census occurs in Palestine under Quirinius around 6–4 BC.	Beginning as a co-ruler with his father, Caesar Tiberius' fifteenth year reign falls about AD 27.
JEWISH KING	Herod dies in 4 BC, after the birth of Jesus.	The forty-sixth year of remodeling on Herod's temple falls around AD 26–27.
GOSPEL WRITERS	Herod kills all two-year-old and younger males in Bethlehem, seeking to kill Jesus (Matt. 2:16).	Jesus enters the next period of New Testament history at about thirty years of age (Luke 3:23).

Though no one knows the exact dates, putting all this information together enables us to approximate when the Private Period of Christ occurred. It begins somewhere between 6 and 4 BC and ends somewhere around AD 26–27, a range of twenty-nine to thirty-three years or, as Luke would say, **about thirty years**. This span not only matches the biblical data but also fits within the historical reigns of the political and religious rulers of that time.

Having examined what, how, where, and when God orchestrates the events of the Private Period of Christ, let's turn our attention to another very important question. Why did God send Jesus?

WHY?

Recall that the main topic of the Bible portrays **God receiving glory by restoring fellowship between humanity and Himself through His Son, Jesus Christ**. Let's look at several examples from this period of New Testament history that underscore God's heart for all nations.

Let's begin by examining the genealogy of Christ found in the very first verses of the New Testament, Matthew 1:1–17. This list of Christ's forbearers reveals something quite interesting about the heart of God. In an unusual act for that day and time, Matthew includes the names of women, not just men. In verses 3–6, Matthew lists the names of four women: Tamar the wife of two of Judah's sons (Genesis 38:6–26), Rahab the prostitute in Jericho who helped Joshua's spies (Joshua 2:1–21), Ruth the great-grandmother of David (Ruth 4:13–22), and Bathsheba the wife of Uriah (2 Samuel 11:2–5). All four women came from Gentile, rather than Jewish, backgrounds. Tamar and Rahab were Canaanites, Ruth was a Moabite, and because Bathsheba's name refers to a pagan god and her husband came from the Hittites, most believe she also came from a Gentile family. Not only does Matthew list the names of Gentiles in the genealogy of Christ, but three of these four women committed acts of immorality. In other words, in these first few verses of the New Testament, God revealed His love for the whole human race—not just male but also female, not just the righteous but also the unrighteous, not just the Jew but also the Gentile.

Recall the night of Jesus' birth. As shepherds watch their sheep, an angel appears to them, making a wonderful announcement. After first exhorting the shepherds not to fear (wouldn't it terribly frighten you if an angel suddenly appeared and the glory of God shone all around you?), the heavenly messenger proclaims that he has good news, and then he explains the glorious arrival of the Savior, Christ the Lord. Notice in Luke 2:10 that the angel meant the good news for "all the people." In other words, God meant the good news not just for Jews but for Gentiles as well. The moment the herald finishes his brief but powerful announcement, a multitude of angels appear. (Perhaps the joyful knowledge of the Savior's birth kept the shepherds from going into cardiac arrest at this point.) This new heavenly host reinforces the concept of God's heart for the nations when they begin praising God for bringing peace "among men" (Luke 2:14).

Six weeks later when Mary and Joseph take Jesus into the temple in order to present Him to the Lord, Simeon intercepts them. Taking baby Jesus into his arms, Simeon makes some startling comments, especially for a devout Jew standing in the middle of the temple. First he rejoices that his eyes have seen God's salvation, and then he quotes from the Old Testament as he identifies Jesus as "a light of revelation to the Gentiles." Isaiah uses this phrase to refer to the coming Messiah as a light for the nations or Gentiles. Isaiah 49:6 says, "I will also make You a light of the nations so that My salvation may reach to the end of the earth." Isaiah 60:3 declares, "And nations will come to your light, and kings to the brightness of your rising." The testimony of Simeon clearly underscores that Jesus' arrival will serve to restore fellowship between God and all the nations of the earth.

Notice that, while both the magi and Herod seek Jesus, it is not the king of the Jews who seeks to worship Jesus but rather the Gentile wise men. We must not forget that these Gentiles traveled a great distance and paid a great price in order to worship the Lord.

SEVEN GROUPS OF PEOPLE	FOCUS ON THE GENTILES
Born to Mary and Joseph	**Gentiles** in Christ's genealogy
Worshiped by the shepherds	Good news for **all the people**
Honored by Simeon and Anna	A light of revelation to the **Gentiles**
Sought by the magi and Herod	Sought by the **Gentile** magi
Taught by temple teachers	In the court of the **Gentiles**
Baptized by John the Baptist	John later identifies Christ as the Lamb of God who takes away the sin of the **world**
Tempted by the devil	Offers Christ a shortcut to the **nations**

No direct link of God's heart for the Gentiles exists in the passage where the temple teachers instruct Jesus. Yet, note that as Jesus listens to the teachers, He sits in the part of the temple called the Court of the Gentiles. When Solomon built and later Zerubbabel rebuilt the temple during Old Testament times, each devoted space for the Gentiles to worship God (see the picture below). Much activity occurred in this area, such as teaching and selling of sacrificial animals by the moneychangers. Nor does the passage about John baptizing Jesus mention anything about God's heart for the Gentiles. However, when Jesus returns six weeks later after His time in the wilderness, John the Baptist describes Jesus as "the Lamb of God who takes away the sin of the world" (John 1:29).

Before leaving this section, let's look again at the devil's temptation of Jesus, a passage that you would not immediately consider as giving evidence of God's heart for the nations. Yet even here we find it. Remember that the devil offers Jesus the kingdoms of the earth. Why would such an offer tempt the Lord of Heaven, the one who originally created the kingdoms? Jesus desires the kingdoms because He came to deliver them from bondage to sin and Satan. He had two options. Either He could purchase them through the shedding of His precious blood, or He could simply bow down and receive them from the devil because they were the devil's to offer. We saw earlier Jesus refusing to take the shortcut. We didn't emphasize, though, the intense desire Christ has for restoring fellowship between God and the nations. This deep motivation makes the offer an attractive temptation.

Herod's Temple

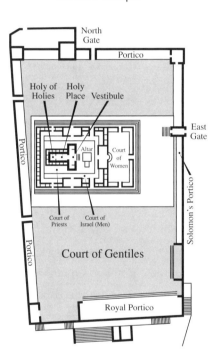

An emphasis on the Gentiles does not begin after Christ's resurrection, as many tend to think. We see it from the beginning of the New Testament. Over and over again in the Private Period of Christ we discover God's heart for all the nations of the earth.

Now let's look at the life of one of the authors of the New Testament.

WHO?

At least eight, possibly nine, authors wrote the twenty-seven books found in the New Testament. (The confusion of number comes from not knowing with certainty who wrote the book of Hebrews. For our purposes we will associate Hebrews with Paul but place a big question mark beside it.) The eight include Matthew, Mark, Luke, John, Peter, Paul, James, and Jude.

We can remember these names easily by recalling that the first four (Matthew, Mark, Luke, and John) are the writers of the four Gospels. The next two, Peter and Paul, represent the two greatest apostles of the New Testament. Scripture identifies the final pair, James and Jude, as half-brothers of Christ.

EIGHT NEW TESTAMENT AUTHORS

4 Authors of the Gospels	Matthew, Mark, Luke, John
2 Pillars of the Church	Peter, Paul
2 Half-brothers of Christ	James, Jude

In this section and every other Who? section in the following chapters, we will study one of the New Testament authors in an effort to master the Word of God. If you also want to grow in your walk with Christ, that is, if you also desire for the Word of God to master you, then visit the website at www.ciu.edu/NTBibleStudy, and scroll down to "Publications." There you will find eight lessons geared for both personal and small group Bible study.

Few verses speak directly about Matthew, only Matthew 9:9; 10:3; Mark 2:14; 3:18; Luke 5:27–29; 6:15; and Acts 1:13. From this small amount of information, however, we know that Matthew, also known as Levi, worked in Capernaum as one of the despised publicans, better known as tax collectors. The Jews hated them because they cooperated with Rome and collected more tax than the Jews actually owed. After Jesus challenges Matthew to follow Him, Matthew hosts a huge party inviting many of his friends, who apparently did not live in a godly manner, so they can meet the Lord. Later Jesus appoints Matthew as one of the twelve disciples.

Matthew's gospel makes many unique contributions to the New Testament. Consider that he, more than any other author, points out how the Lord Jesus fulfills Old Testament prophecies of the coming Messiah. Another unique contribution of Matthew involves his focus on the spoken words of Jesus. The book of Matthew contains five major sermons of the Lord Jesus, each one ending with the phrase "when Jesus had finished these words." The five sermons include the famous Sermon on the Mount (chapters 5–7), instructions for the twelve disciples (chapter 10), parables about the kingdom of heaven (chapter 13), a message on discipleship (chapter 18), and finally what we call the Olivet Discourse (chapters 24–25).

FOR NEXT TIME

If you are having an extremely busy week:	If you have a little extra time:	If you can't get enough:
read Mark 1–9.	add John 1–4; Mark 1–9; John 7–11.	add John 1–4; Mark 1–2; John 5; Mark 3–9; John 7–8; Luke 10–12; John 9–10; Luke 14–16; John 11; Mark 10.

(Note that the order of the reading is chronologically arranged.)

PERIOD #2

PERIOD #2

Christ's Public Period

In the Introduction, we learned that we can divide the New Testament into two historical eras, which we can, in turn, subdivide into eight periods. To plant this organizational structure deeply within your mind, you will have the opportunity at the beginning of each chapter to review. Fill in the following chart, and see how you do.

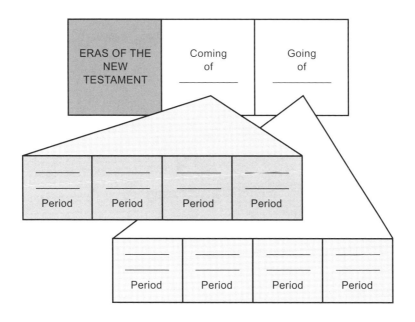

In chapter one we examined the first of these eight periods, which focuses on the preparation of the Messiah. Seven groups of people summarize the events that occur during this initial unit of time. Fill in the chart below with the names of each group.

SEVEN GROUPS OF PEOPLE

	MATTHEW	LUKE
Born to _____ and _____	1:1–25	1:1–2:7
Worshiped by the _____		2:8–2:21
Honored by _____ and _____		2:22–40
Sought by the _____ and _____	2:1–23	
Taught by temple _____		2:41–52
Baptized by _____	3:1–17	3:1–38
Tempted by the _____	4:1–11	4:1–13

After years spent in obscurity during the Private Period, Christ quietly begins a new phase of His ministry. Though He starts His Public Period relatively unnoticed, it doesn't end that way. Let's see what happens.

WHAT?

Each of the four Gospels devotes quite a few chapters to the Public Period of Christ as you can see in the chart below.

CHRIST'S PUBLIC PERIOD

Matthew	Mark	Luke	John
16 ½ chapters	9 ½ chapters	15 chapters	11 chapters
(4:12–20:34)	(1:14–10:52)	(4:14–19:27)	(1:19–12:11)

But what main emphasis occurs during this second period of the Coming Era? Whereas the Private Period of Christ focuses on the preparation of the Messiah, the Public Period of Christ focuses on **the proclamation of the Messiah**. During this time period the Lord communicates that God has manifested His love and forgiveness for the nations by sending Jesus as the long-awaited Messiah. Though the nations, both Jew and Gentile, live in disobedience to God's laws, they can appropriate God's forgiveness by trusting Christ (as opposed to their good works) to make them right with God.

Let's now look at how the Lord Jesus specifically goes about proclaiming God's love and forgiveness to the nations during His public ministry.

HOW?

If you read only one of the four Gospels, you will not gain the full picture of what happened during this time frame. Each author adds something important that the others do not. Even if we read all four Gospels consecutively, we may not capture the flow of the story. Two factors create this unfortunate reality. First, each book contains so many unique events that we lose the flow of the overall story. Second, Matthew arranges the material in his gospel topically, rather than chronologically like the others. Not realizing this difference may make you wonder about the correct order of the events.

We can arrange the four Gospels in such a way, however, as to read them as one continuous story without duplicating many of the events. For a simple harmonized story of the Public Period of Christ, read these chapters in this order: John 1–4, Mark 1–2, John 5, Mark 3–9, John 7–11, Mark 10, and the first half of John 12. Notice that we read only from the Gospels of Mark and John. We include Mark because it represents the simplest of the Synoptic Gospels. The word *synoptic*, meaning "the common view," is often used to describe the books of Matthew, Mark, and Luke because they are similar in their approaches to telling their story, especially when compared with the Gospel of John. So, adding the chapters from John provides us with a well-informed view of this New Testament time period.

The following chart summarizes fifty-six main episodes in the story of Christ's public ministry.

OVERVIEW OF THE PUBLIC PERIOD OF CHRIST

1	John 1:1–18	The Son of God becomes man so that sinful men can become sons of God.
2	John 1:19–34	When Jesus returns to Bethany, the place of His baptism, from His temptation in the wilderness, John the Baptist identifies Jesus as the Lamb of God who takes away the sin of the world.
3	John 1:35–51	While in Bethany Jesus calls Andrew, John, Peter, Philip, and Nathanael to follow Him.
4	John 2:1–12	Jesus takes a several-day trip with His disciples to a wedding in the city of Cana in Galilee, where He performs His first miracle: turning water into wine. After the wedding, Jesus travels with His disciples and family to Capernaum, another city in Galilee.
5	John 2:13–25	Jesus returns to Jerusalem in Judea for the Passover, where He cleanses the temple of moneychangers and hints at His future resurrection.
6	John 3:1–21	Still in Jerusalem, Jesus explains to Nicodemus that in order to be right with God a person must be born again.
7	John 3:22–36	Leaving Jerusalem, Jesus spends time with His disciples in the region of Judea, where they baptize people.

8	John 4:1–42	Pressure from the religious authorities motivates Jesus to leave Judea for Galilee. As He passes through Samaria, He stops in the city of Sychar and explains to a woman at the well that He is living water, the Messiah.
9	John 4:43–54	Jesus arrives in Galilee, stopping first at Cana. While in Cana, He heals a royal official's son, who is sick with a fever in the city of Capernaum, located on the northwestern shore of the Sea of Galilee. As a result, the official and his household believe in Jesus. Jesus then travels by way of Nazareth to Capernaum (Luke 4:16, 31), which becomes His base of operations in Galilee (Matt. 4:13).
10	Mark 1:14–20	Jesus sees Peter, Andrew, James, and John fishing in the Sea of Galilee and calls them to follow Him on a full-time basis. Jesus invites people to believe in the gospel.
11	Mark 1:21–34	On a Sabbath, Jesus teaches in the synagogue of the city of Capernaum. After teaching, He casts a demon out of a man inside the synagogue. Later that day Jesus visits the home of Peter and Andrew, where He heals Peter's mother-in-law. As evening arrives, "the whole city" comes to the house, where Jesus heals many of their sick and casts out many demons.
12	Mark 1:35–39	Early the next morning Jesus finds a secluded place to pray. When Peter and the others find the Lord, He announces that He came to preach the gospel (see Mark 1:14). They depart for nearby towns where Jesus preaches and casts out demons in the various synagogues.
13	Mark 1:40–45	While on this ministry trip Jesus also heals a leper.
14	Mark 2:1–12	Back in Capernaum Jesus forgives a paralytic's sins. When the scribes accuse Him of blasphemy, He proves He is the Son of Man (the Messiah) by healing the man.
15	Mark 2:13–17	Jesus calls Matthew, a tax collector in Capernaum, to follow Him and then attends a big reception (Luke 5:29) that Matthew gives for Him.

16	Mark 2:18–28	Still in Capernaum, Jesus uses three parables to explain to the Pharisees and others why His disciples do not fast while He remains with them.
17	John 5:1–9	Jesus visits Jerusalem in Judea during one of the feasts, where He heals a lame man on the Sabbath at the Pool of Bethesda.
18	John 5:10–47	The Pharisees in Jerusalem want to kill Jesus because He heals the lame man on the Sabbath and makes Himself equal with God by claiming God as His Father.
19	Mark 3:1–6	Back in Galilee, Jesus heals a man's withered hand. Upset because the healing occurs on a Sabbath, the Pharisees plot with the Herodians how they might destroy Jesus.
20	Mark 3:7–12	Jesus withdraws to the Sea of Galilee with His disciples. A great multitude from all over Palestine follows Him because He has healed many and cast out many demons.
21	Mark 3:13–19	At a nearby mountain, Jesus appoints the twelve disciples to be with Him so that He might send them out to preach. He then gives the famous Sermon on the Mount (Luke 6:12–49).
22	Mark 3:20–35	Upon His return home to Capernaum, the multitudes surround Him such that He cannot even eat. Scribes arriving from Jerusalem announce that Beelzebub (Satan, the ruler of the demons) gives Jesus His power to cast out demons.
23	Mark 4:1–34	Speaking from a boat off the shore of the Sea of Galilee, Jesus teaches a great multitude using parables. He explains the meaning of the parables privately to His disciples.
24	Mark 4:35–41	That evening as the disciples take Jesus to the other side of the Sea of Galilee, a fierce storm arises, threatening the lives of all in the boat. The fearful disciples wake the sleeping Lord who miraculously calms the wind and the waves with a simple command.

25	Mark 5:1–20	Now on the Gerasenes side, or east side, of the Sea of Galilee, Jesus casts out a large number of demons from one man and sends them into a herd of swine.
26	Mark 5:21–43	Traveling back across the Sea of Galilee to Capernaum, Jesus heals a woman who touches the fringe of His garment and raises from the dead the daughter of Jairus, the synagogue official.
27	Mark 6:1–6	Jesus goes to His hometown of Nazareth and heals only a few due to their unbelief. They consider Him nothing more than the brother of James, Joses, Judas, Simon, and His sisters.
28	Mark 6:7–31	Somewhere in Galilee Jesus instructs the Twelve and sends them out to preach to the Jews that they should repent.
29	Mark 6:32–44	At the time of the Passover (John 6:4–13), the Lord travels with the twelve disciples by boat to Bethsaida (Luke 9:10), located on the north shore of the Sea of Galilee along the Jordan River, and then walks to a secluded place. The multitudes follow. At the end of the day Jesus feeds 5,000 men plus women and children, using only five loaves of bread and two fish.
30	Mark 6:45–52	Sending His disciples away by boat toward Bethsaida and Capernaum (John 6:16–18), Jesus remains that evening to pray. About 3 A.M. the next morning, He walks three or four miles (John 6:19) on the surface of the water to the boat.
31	Mark 6:53–56	Landing on the western shore of the Sea of Galilee at Gennesaret, Jesus goes about the various villages and cities healing the sick.
32	Mark 7:1–23	Pharisees and scribes from Jerusalem find Jesus in Galilee and argue with Him about what defiles a person. Afterward Jesus uses a parable to tell the multitude that inner, not outer, dirt defiles a person.

33	Mark 7:24–30	They travel to an area near Tyre, a (Gentile) city in the region of Phoenicia, located north of Galilee on the Mediterranean seacoast. There Jesus casts a demon out of a Syrophoenician woman's daughter.
34	Mark 7:31–37	Next Jesus travels via Sidon to the region of Decapolis (east of Samaria across the Jordan River) along the southeastern coast of the Sea of Galilee and heals a man's deafness and speech impediment.
35	Mark 8:1–9	In Decapolis, Jesus feeds a multitude numbering 4,000 by multiplying seven loaves of bread and a few small fish.
36	Mark 8:10–21	Jesus travels by boat to Dalmanutha, an area on the western coast of the Sea of Galilee near Magadan. The Pharisees come to Jesus and once again argue with Him. Leaving by boat for the other side of the Sea of Galilee, the Lord warns His disciples about the Pharisees.
37	Mark 8:22–26	Landing by boat in Bethsaida, Jesus heals a blind man.
38	Mark 8:27–9:1	Traveling with His disciples to the villages surrounding Caesarea Philippi (Matt. 16:13), a city north of the Sea of Galilee in the region of Iturea, Jesus asks who people think He is. Peter declares that Jesus is the Christ, the Messiah. Jesus then teaches His disciples about His coming death and resurrection.
39	Mark 9:2–13	Six days later, on a high mountain near Caesarea Philippi, Peter, James, and John watch as Jesus transfigures and powerfully reveals the kingdom of God (see Mark 9:1). Then the three hear God proclaim, "This is My beloved Son, listen to Him!"
40	Mark 9:14–29	Coming down from the mountain, Jesus casts out a demon and teaches His disciples about prayer and fasting.

41	Mark 9:30–50	Walking from Caesarea Philippi through Galilee, Jesus teaches His disciples about His coming death and resurrection. Arriving in Capernaum, He instructs them about servanthood and hell.
42	John 7:1–53	Jesus walks to Jerusalem to participate in the Feast of Booths, also known as the Feast of Tabernacles. As He teaches in the temple, many of the multitude believe that Jesus is the Christ. The Pharisees, however, send officers to seize Him. The officers choose not to seize Him because His teaching amazes them.
43	John 8:1–59	After spending the night on the Mount of Olives outside Jerusalem, Jesus returns to the temple. As He teaches the crowds, the scribes and Pharisees bring Him a woman caught in adultery, and He forgives her sin. As He continues teaching, many believe in Him. When He claims deity (implied when He says, "I am"; see Ex. 3:14), some of those listening attempt to stone Him.
44	John 9:1–41	Later Jesus returns on a Sabbath to Jerusalem and heals a man born blind. After healing the man, Jesus introduces Himself as the Son of Man, an Old Testament title referring to the Messiah.
45	John 10:1–21	Jesus tells those listening that, as the Good Shepherd, He will lay His life down for the sheep.
46	John 10:22–39	During the winter Jesus returns to Jerusalem to participate in the Feast of Dedication, also known as the Feast of Lights or Hanukkah. The Jews ask Jesus to tell them plainly if He is the Christ. When He tells them that He and the Father are One, they seek to stone Him for claiming to be the Son of God. He escapes their attempt.
47	John 10:40–42	Leaving Jerusalem, Jesus goes across the Jordan River into the region of Perea, where many believe in Him.

48	John 11:1–44	News reaches Jesus while in Perea that Lazarus, one of His friends, has died. He returns to the Judean Bethany located two miles from Jerusalem and raises Lazarus from the dead.
49	John 11:45–53	After Jesus raises Lazarus from the dead, the Pharisees in Jerusalem begin to plot to kill Him, fearing that many more might believe in Him thus causing the Romans to come and take away both their place and nation.
50	John 11:54–57	Jesus and His disciples retreat to the city of Ephraim near the Judean wilderness. Back in Jerusalem the chief priests and Pharisees give the order that anyone knowing the location of Jesus should report it so that they might seize Him.
51	Mark 10:1–16	Jesus moves once again into the region of Perea beyond the Jordan River and teaches the crowds. He also explains marriage and divorce to some Pharisees who test Him.
52	Mark 10:17–31	In Perea, after talking to a rich young ruler, Jesus explains to His disciples that a man cannot enter the kingdom of God by his own efforts. Only God could let someone into His kingdom.
53	Mark 10:32–34	Traveling through Judea back to Jerusalem for the Passover, Jesus again tells the Twelve that He will be scourged and killed but three days later will rise again.
54	Mark 10:35–45	On the journey back to Jerusalem, Jesus explains to the Twelve that the Son of Man did not come to be served but to serve and to give His life as a ransom for many.
55	Mark 10:46–52	Reaching Jericho Jesus heals a blind man named Bartimaeus who calls out to Jesus as the Son of David, another Old Testament title for the Messiah.
56	John 12:1–11	Six days before the Passover, Jesus and the Twelve finish their journey at Bethany, outside of Jerusalem, and come to the home of Lazarus and his two sisters, Mary and Martha. A great multitude learns of His arrival and comes to Him, which results in many believing in Him.

In order to remember the important events that occured during the Public Period of Christ, we simply need to spend a few moments memorizing the fifty-six items above! If that seems a bit daunting, then let's organize the fifty-six items into various categories. We summarized the Private Period of Christ with seven groups of people, and we can gather the events of the Public Period of Christ into **seven themes** about the Messiah.

Notice that almost all of the fifty-six events deal with one or more of the following themes: Jesus teaching the multitudes; Jesus training His disciples; Jesus being criticized by the religious leaders; Jesus performing miracles; Jesus healing the sick; Jesus delivering people from demons; and, last but most importantly, Jesus explaining how people can be made right with God by believing in Him as the Messiah.

To increase your confidence that these seven themes accurately capture the vast majority of what takes place during the Public Period of Christ, take a few minutes to complete the following exercise. The chart below lists the seven themes in the left column. The right column has been left blank so you can list the number of each of the fifty-six events next to the theme it best represents. You may need to list some of the events in more than one theme because the event may have multiple activities, such as Jesus healing the sick as well as casting out demons. To get you started, the first seven events have already been entered on the chart. Do not feel obligated to categorize all fifty-six events, only enough to assure yourself that these seven themes summarize this period in the life of Christ.

THEME	EVENT NUMBER
Inspires the multitudes	
Instructs the Twelve	3, 7
Infuriates the Pharisees	
Causes miracles	4
Cures the sick	
Casts out demons	
Reveals that we can be made right with God	1, 2, 5, 6

Recalling seven themes still requires a little bit of effort. In order to maximize our memory, let's further arrange these seven themes around Jesus' sayings, Jesus' actions, and Jesus' purpose. Or as we put it in the chart below: the words, works, and way of Christ. We arranged the chart with the "Way of Christ" at the bottom in order to represent Christ's mission as the foundation of all He said and did.

THE WORDS OF CHRIST	THE WORKS OF CHRIST
Inspires the multitudes	Causes miracles
Instructs the Twelve	Cures the sick
Infuriates the Pharisees	Casts out demons
THE WAY OF CHRIST	
Reveals that we can be made right with God by believing in Him as the Messiah	

Now that we have a better understanding of fifty-six events that occurred during this period, let's look at where everything takes place.

WHERE?

Before determining the location of the above fifty-six events, we need to understand the bigger geographical picture. As you recall, during the time of Jesus, the Roman Empire ruled the Western world encircling the Mediterranean Sea. For administrative purposes, the Empire divided their conquered territories into various provinces, as you can see on the map that follows.

Organization of the Roman Empire

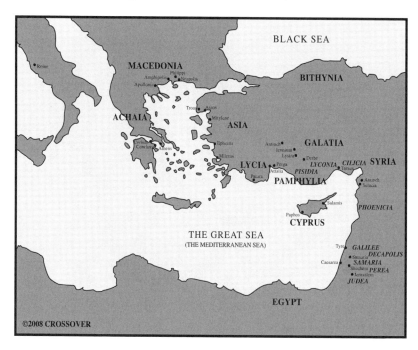

The land of Palestine falls within the province of Syria. Palestine further divides into five districts: Judea, Samaria, Galilee, Decapolis, and Perea.

The Five Districts of Palestine

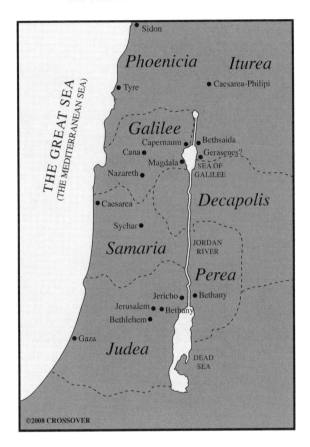

Jesus spends time in each of the five districts of Palestine. He also takes trips into the districts of Phoenicia and Iturea, both lying north of Galilee. Yet the vast amount of His activity occurs in Judea and Galilee.

We can now place each of the fifty-six events in their proper geographical context. The chart below shows in which district each event occurs. To better comprehend the movement of Jesus during this Public Period, read again each key event from the chart on pages 46 to 52. You should find enough information to determine where each event took place. As you discover the district, write it in the left margin beside the event's number. If you have difficulty, refer to the chart below for help. Personally determining the geography will pay large dividends as you seek to put together the puzzle of the New Testament.

EVENT NUMBER	REGION
1	n/a
2–3	Perea
4	Galilee
5–7	Judea
8	Samaria
9–16	Galilee
17–18	Judea
19–32	Galilee
33	Phoenicia
34–35	Decapolis
36–37	Galilee
38–40	Iturea
41	Galilee
42–46	Judea
47	Perea
48–50	Judea
51–52	Perea
53–56	Judea

Tracing the movement of Jesus during this period, as in the previous period, shows Him traveling the length of Palestine several times. Most of Jesus' ministry, however, occurs in Galilee, far away from the religious leaders of Jerusalem who seek to persecute Him. Out of the spotlight, Jesus concentrates on developing the twelve disciples, who will take the message of God's love and forgiveness to the nations after He ascends into heaven.

While in Galilee, Jesus makes **Capernaum** His center of ministry. Matthew 4:13 speaks of Jesus settling in Capernaum. Not only does He always return to Capernaum after long ministry trips but He also performs many of His key works in that city: healing a royal official's son; casting the demon out of a man in the Capernaum synagogue; healing Peter's mother-in-law; healing many of the city's sick and demon possessed; forgiving and healing a paralytic; calling Matthew to follow Him; defending Himself against the accusation that Beelzebub gave Him authority to cast out demons; healing a hemorrhaging woman; healing the daughter of the synagogue official; and teaching His disciples many spiritual lessons.

Having answered the question of where the seven themes occurred during the Public Period of Christ, let's learn when they take place.

WHEN?

If Christ's Private Period ends around AD 26–27, we know that the current period begins at the same time. When, however, does this Public Period end? From the last key event found above, number fifty-six, we know generally that Jesus arrives in Jerusalem six days before the Passover on which the Romans crucify Him. Yet when specifically does this Passover occur? To answer this question we must determine the day of the week, the date of the month, and the actual year of His crucifixion.

Let's begin with which day of the week the crucifixion takes place. All four Gospels (Matthew 27:62; Mark 15:42; Luke 23:54; John 19:31, 42) mention that the crucifixion of Jesus occurs on the Jewish day of preparation, which we know as Friday.

Now as to the date of the month, we must think in terms of the Jewish calendar, not our own calendar. According to Exodus 12:1–4, Passover occurs every year on the fourteenth day of the first month. The

Jewish calendar initially gives the name *Abib* (Deuteronomy 16:1) to the first month and later changes its name to *Nisan* (Nehemiah 2:1). The chart below shows how the Jewish calendar generally compares to the calendar we use today.

JEWISH CALENDAR	OUR CALENDAR
Nisan (or Abib)	March/April
Iyyar	April/May
Sivan	May/June
Tammuz	June/July
Ab	July/August
Ilul	August/September
Tishri	September/October
Marhesvan	October/November
Kislev	November/December
Tebeth	December/January
Shebat	January/February
Adar	February/March

John 18:28 tells us that when the Jewish leaders take Jesus to Pilate, they chose not to enter the Praetorium so they could remain undefiled in order to eat the Passover meal that night. So John lets us know that the crucifixion occurs on the day of the Passover, Nisan 14.

In the previous chapter, we saw that Pilate governed from AD 26–36. During his rule, Nisan 14 fell on a Friday twice: in AD 30 and AD 33. Which of these dates do we choose? It depends on how long the Public Period lasts. If it lasts around three years, we choose the former date. If, however, it seems to last around six years, we select the latter.

Using the number of Passover Feasts mentioned in the Gospels as a guide, most historians believe the ministry of Jesus extends a full three years and part of another. The partial year occurs between Jesus' wilderness experience and the Passover Feast John mentions in John 2:13. The first full year of his ministry goes from this Passover to the next Passover, which may be the "feast of the Jews" found in John 5:1. The second full year takes place between the possible Passover at which John 5:1 hints and the one clearly mentioned in John 6:4. The final full year of ministry ends with the Passover highlighted in John 12:1, the one during which the Romans crucify Jesus.

Let's assemble our evidence. We know Jesus dies on Nisan 14, which falls on a Friday. We know that while Pontius Pilate governs in Judea, Nisan 14 falls on a Friday twice: in AD 30 and AD 33. Additionally, we know that Jesus' ministry lasts only a little more than three years. Because we also know that the Public Period of Christ begins around AD 26 or AD 27, we can conclude that Jesus dies in AD 30. Now we do not want to become dogmatic about our conclusion, because others make a strong case for the crucifixion occurring during AD 33; but from the biblical and historical data we have considered, our resulting decision appears free of any major difficulties.

Before leaving this section, let's consider one other helpful aspect about the feasts. Not only do they allow us to approximate the duration of Jesus' ministry but also they give us a general idea of when each of the fifty-six key events take place. In addition to writing about the Passovers, which fall around March or April, John also writes once (or twice) about the Feast of Tabernacles (also known as the Feast of Booths), celebrated each year around October (John 5:1; 7:2), and the Feast of Dedication, which occurs around December (John 10:22). Using the feast in John 5:1 as a Passover, the chart below helps us visualize the chronological flow of Jesus' ministry.

As you did during the Where? section, you may want to return to the chart (pages 46 to 52) that lists the fifty-six key events occurring during this period and write in the right margin the year and approximate season of each event. The chart below will help you determine the approximate dates. For example, beside key event 5, you would write March/April AD 27. Beside events 6–16, you would write May AD 27 to March AD 28.

Taking the time to complete this exercise will help you understand the chronological flow of Jesus' ministry.

	AD 27	AD 28	AD 29	AD 30
JANUARY TO MARCH	Events 2–4	Events 6–16	Events 19–28	Events 47–56
APRIL	Feast of Passover (John 2:13)	Possibly, Feast of Passover (John 5:1)	Feast of Passover (John 6:4)	Feast of Passover (John 12:1)
MAY				
JUNE				
JULY			Events 30–41	
AUGUST				
SEPTEMBER	Events 6–16	Events 19–28		
OCTOBER			Feast of Tabernacles (John 7:2)	
NOVEMBER			Events 43–45	
DECEMBER			Feast of Dedication (John 10:22)	

In summary, we now know that the Public Period of Christ begins around AD 26–27 and ends six days before the Passover that occurs on Friday, Nisan 14, AD 30, for a total of about **three and a half years**. We turn our attention, at this point, to the Why? question.

WHY?

We must always keep in mind the driving force or theme of the whole Bible: **God receiving glory by restoring fellowship between all people groups and Himself through His Son, Jesus Christ.** During the

Public Period of biblical history, Jesus launches His ministry by proclaiming that believing in Him would restore fellowship with God. To whom, however, did Jesus announce this message? Though He focuses on Jews, He does not limit Himself to Jews. From the beginning, Jesus declares God's love to all people groups. Three passages from this period of the New Testament show us that He issues His proclamation of forgiveness to Jews, Samaritans, and Gentiles.

In the first passage, the third chapter of the Gospel of John, we find Jesus talking one night in Jerusalem to Nicodemus, a very important Jew. Nicodemus serves as a member of the Sanhedrin, the governing body for the religious affairs and, under Roman oversight, the civil life of the Jews. As they talk, Nicodemus acknowledges that Jesus has come from God as a teacher. Jesus quickly moves the conversation to the real question—how Nicodemus could enter the kingdom of God. Jesus declares the answer in John 3:15, "Whoever believes may in Him have eternal life." Jesus then summarizes the whole theme of the Bible in such a simple yet powerful manner that the verse, John 3:16, has become one of the most famous passages of Scripture in the entire world: "For God so loved the world, that He gave His only begotten Son, that whoever believes in Him should not perish, but have eternal life." It appears that Nicodemus trusts in Christ, because he helps with the burial of Jesus in John 19:39, an action completely contrary to the decision of the Sanhedrin. Although Jesus addresses His comment to a Jew, notice that He uses the words *world* and *whoever*, meaning that anyone—Jew, Samaritan, or Gentile—would have eternal life if he or she simply trusts in Christ to become right with God.

Jesus in John 3 proclaims God's love and forgiveness to a Jew, and in John 4 He communicates the same message to a Samaritan. During this time in history, people could choose from various Roman roads to travel from Judea to Galilee (see the following map). The first road, running along the Mediterranean seacoast, took travelers too far out of the way. Most people chose the road which ran near the region of Perea, even though a different road proved the shortest. They avoided the most direct route because of the danger the Samaritans represented. As neither Jews nor Gentiles, the Samaritans originated from the intermarrying of Jews and Gentiles after the Assyrians conquered the northern kingdom of Israel in 722 BC. They differed from the Jews religiously in that they had only the first five books of the Old Testament and believed people should worship God at Mount Gerizim rather than Jerusalem. Resenting Jewish prejudice, the Samaritans often caused harm to travelers from Judea.

Roman Roads in Palestine

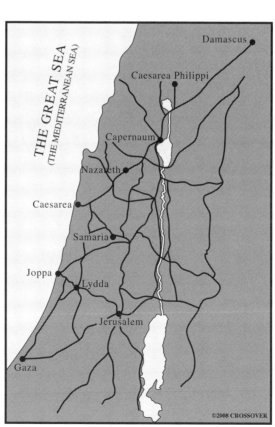

With this in mind, notice that in John 4:4 Jesus *has to pass* through Samaria. He has to go through Samaria, not for physical reasons, but for spiritual reasons. A divine appointment awaits Him in the Samaritan city of Sychar. Arriving in Sychar around noon, Jesus meets an immoral Samaritan woman at the ancient well of Jacob. As they talk, she suspects He may be the promised Messiah. Even though Samaritans had only the first five books of the Old Testament, they had enough of Scripture to know about the prophesied Messiah. Perhaps her knowledge of Deuteronomy 18:18 prompts her to call Jesus a prophet in John 4:19. When the unnamed woman mentions the coming Messiah, Jesus confirms that He is the Christ.

The woman becomes so excited that she leaves her water pot in order to race into town to tell everyone that she had found the Christ. As a result, many other Samaritans believe in Jesus to make them right with God (John 4:39). Notice in verse 42 that the Samaritans come to know Jesus as "the Savior of the world." Again, not only Jews and Samaritans but also the world could know God's love and forgiveness.

Before moving to the third passage, consider the stark differences between Nicodemus and the woman at the well, yet the similar need of each to be right with God.

	NICODEMUS	WOMAN AT THE WELL
NATIONALITY	Jewish	Samaritan
GENDER	Male	Female
NAME	Named	Unnamed
MORALITY	Moral	Immoral
CHRIST'S OFFER	To be born spiritually	To receive Living Water
LESSON	He couldn't be good enough to get himself into heaven.	She couldn't be bad enough to keep herself out of heaven.

In the land of the Jews, Jesus proclaims God's love and forgiveness to the Jews. In the region of the Samaritans, Jesus announces God's love and forgiveness to the Samaritans. In the third passage we find Jesus in the land of the Gentiles. Let's see what he communicates to the Gentiles. In key event 33 in the How? section, we find Jesus traveling to the region of Tyre, the Gentile city of the Phoenicians. Both Mark 7:26–30 and Matthew 15:21–28 record this event, but because Matthew adds more detail we will focus on that passage.

While He travels in the district of Tyre and Sidon, Jesus is approached by a woman. Matthew characterizes her as a "Canaanite," the Old Testament term given to all the various Gentile people groups living in the Promised Land before the Hebrews occupied it. She comes to Jesus because a demon has possessed her daughter, and she wants Him to deliver her. Jesus' response seems unusual in light of all we've learned about God's love for the Gentiles. He initially ignores her. When she persists, He compares her to a dog, which Jewish culture of that day considered a slur. Finally, after she refuses to leave, He commends her for her great faith and heals her daughter at once.

Two questions need answering. First, because faith must always have an object, in what did the woman place her great faith? We discover the answer in Matthew 15:22. The woman addresses Jesus as the Son of David, the same title by which blind Bartimaeus addresses Jesus in key event 55. Such a title refers to the promised Messiah. The Gentile woman had placed her faith in Jesus as the Christ.

	REPRESENTATIVE	CALLS JESUS
GOOD NEWS FOR JEWS IN JOHN 3	Nicodemus	Teacher sent from God (v. 2)
GOOD NEWS FOR SAMARITANS IN JOHN 4	Woman at the well	Prophet (v. 19), Christ (v. 29; see also v. 25)
GOOD NEWS FOR GENTILES IN MATTHEW 15	Canaanite woman	Lord, Son of David (v. 22)

Why then did Jesus initially act in such a seemingly unkind, contradictory manner toward the Canaanite woman? We find the answer in the attitude of the disciples as they repeatedly ask the Lord to send the woman away. Recall that God told Abraham He would bless him *so that* he and his offspring would be a blessing to all the nations of the earth. Unfortunately, the people of God in the Old Testament kept forgetting the "so that," going as far as to develop contempt for Gentiles. The disciples of Jesus, at this point in their training, reflect the same cultural animosity toward Gentiles.

As the master teacher, Jesus knew how to get a person's attention. In the story of the woman at the well, Jesus tells His disciples—after they walk all the way to town in order to bring Jesus food—that He already has food to eat. Once He has their attention He tells them that doing the will of God gives Him nourishment. In this passage about the Canaanite woman Jesus initially imitates His culture's self-centeredness in order to get the attention of the disciples. By later blessing the woman and commending her great faith, He powerfully contrasts the difference between His love and theirs. He pointedly reminds His followers once again that He had come to proclaim God's love and forgiveness not just to the Jew but to the Gentile as well.

Let's now turn our attention to the second of the eight New Testament authors.

WHO?

In the last chapter we focused on Matthew, the first of eight authors of the New Testament. Here we shall consider Mark. Only ten direct references speak about this second writer of the New Testament: Acts 12:12, 25; 13:5; 13:13; 15:37, 39; Colossians 4:10; Philemon 24; 2 Timothy 4:11; and 1 Peter 5:13. Many historians add Mark 14:51–52 as another indirect autobiographical reference about this second New Testament author. Let's see what we learn about Mark from these eleven verses.

If Mark writes about himself when describing the young man who escapes naked in Mark 14:51–52, then he witnesses the arrest of Jesus in the garden of Gethsemane. The first direct reference, however, occurs about fourteen years after the crucifixion. Acts 12 tells the story of the apostle Peter miraculously escaping from a Jerusalem prison after having been incarcerated by Herod Agrippa. Peter goes directly to the house of Mary, the mother of John Mark (v. 12), where he seems to expect to find believers. This passage provides insight into Mark's background. It reveals that he came from a wealthy family because of the size of his mother's house, with its upper room, outer gate, and servant. Some believe John Mark's house possibly served as the location of the last supper of Jesus with His disciples and/or the upper room where the disciples prayed at Pentecost.

Shortly after this event Mark accompanies his cousin Barnabas and the apostle Paul to Antioch, Syria (Acts 12:25). A couple of years later Mark accompanies Barnabas and Paul on a missionary trip to Asia Minor to serve as a helper (Acts 13:5), but he deserts them (Acts 13:13). A few years later in the early 50s, when Barnabas wants to take Mark with him on a second missionary trip (Acts 15:37–39), Paul refuses to let Mark accompany them; and this results in Paul going to Asia Minor and Barnabas taking Mark to minister on the island of Cyprus.

At some point Mark and Paul reconcile their relationship, because we find Mark with Paul in Rome during Paul's house arrest in the early 60s (Colossians 4:10; Philemon 24). In the years just before the house arrest, Mark writes his fast-moving, action-packed gospel (he uses the word *immediately* over forty times) from the same city. Not long after Paul's house arrest, the apostle Peter writes his first epistle from Rome in which he mentions Mark's presence (1 Peter 5:13) and refers to him as his son, suggesting that Peter may have led Mark to place his faith in Christ.

The last reference that refers to Mark (2 Timothy 4:11) comes at the end of the apostle Paul's life when he requests Timothy and Mark to come see him in prison before the Romans execute him.

FOR NEXT TIME

If you are having an extremely busy week:	If you have a little extra time:	If you can't get enough:
read Luke 19–23.	add John 12–19.	add Matthew 21–27 and Mark 11–15.

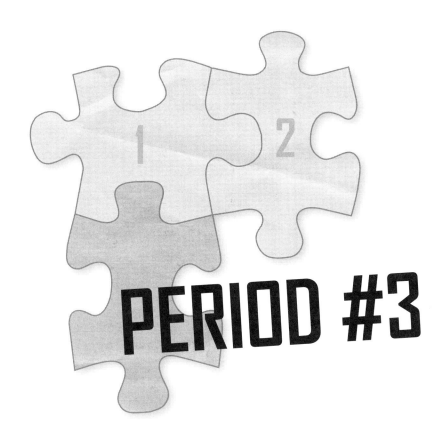

PERIOD #3

PERIOD #3

Christ's Trials Period

As we put together the puzzle of the New Testament, we want to keep in mind the framework of the picture. So let's take time to review once again what we have learned to this point. In the chart below fill in the two missing eras and the corresponding eight periods of New Testament history.

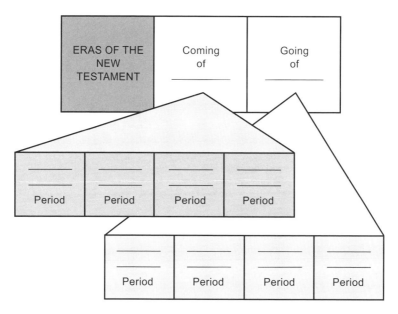

We found that seven groups of people summarize the events that occurred during this Private Period of Christ, and then we discovered that seven themes characterize the Public Period of Christ. Fill in the chart below with both the groups and the themes. If the themes do not come immediately to mind, perhaps this clue will help. Think of Christ's words, works, and way. If this hint does not sufficiently help, turn to the chart on page 54 for the answers.

PERIOD #1 SEVEN GROUPS	PERIOD #2 SEVEN THEMES
Born to _____ and _____	Inspires the _____
Worshiped by the _____	Instructs the _____
Honored by _____ and _____	Infuriates the _____
Sought by the _____ and _____	Causes _____
Taught by temple _____	Cures the _____
Baptized by _____	Casts out _____
Tempted by the _____	Reveals that we can be _____

In the previous chapter on the Public Period of Christ, we left Jesus at the home of Lazarus, Martha, and Mary in Bethany, two miles outside of Jerusalem, six days before the Passover. Having finished the three-plus years of his public ministry, our Lord now begins the third and most difficult period of the Coming of Christ Era.

WHAT?

For thousands of years the Old Testament promised the coming of the Messiah, one who would deliver His people from sin and Satan. When Jesus finally arrives, He spends thirty private years preparing for His three and a half years of public ministry, during which He proclaims God's love and forgiveness to the nations, especially to the Jews. Yet the public ministry of Jesus does not ultimately qualify Him as the Christ, neither does His divinity nor His perfect life, though all three stand as necessary prerequisites.

The determining factor proves much more painful, for ultimately the Messiah has to die to pay for the sins of the world. The people of God understood this concept. God had communicated it since the beginning of Scripture (Genesis 9:4), clearly articulating the concept in Leviticus 17:11–14, when God told Moses, "For the life of the flesh is in the blood, and I have given it to you on the altar to make atonement [payment] for your souls; for it is the blood by reason of the life that makes atonement." Or as Hebrews 9:22 put it, "And without shedding of blood there is no forgiveness." Only death could satisfy God's holy law and clear the way for the nations to gain access to God. And Jesus does just that.

This third period of New Testament history focuses on the suffering or **the persecution of the Messiah.** We call this time frame the Trials Period of Christ because of the painful ordeal He endures as well as to remind us of the six actual trials He experiences. Though the time period lasts only a week, each Gospel writer devotes a number of chapters to these final days in the life of Jesus.

CHRIST'S TRIALS PERIOD

Matthew	Mark	Luke	John
7 chapters	5 chapters	4 ½ chapters	7 ½ chapters
(21:1–27:66)	(11:1–15:47)	(19:28–23:56)	(12:12–19:42)

We gain perspective on the importance of this period by noticing the amount of attention the Gospel writers devote to these seven days, compared to the number of chapters they devote to the other two time periods.

COMING OF CHRIST ERA

	TOTAL TIME	TOTAL CHAPTERS
Private Period	≈ 30 years	8
Public Period	≈ 3 ½ years	52
Trials Period	7 days	24

In his first letter, Peter states, "For Christ also died for sins once for all, the just for the unjust, in order that He might bring us to God, having been put to death in the flesh, but made alive in the spirit" (1 Peter 3:18). Focus now on how Jesus accomplishes this glorious work of bringing the nations to God.

HOW?

Recall that we organized the events of the Private Period of Christ around seven groups of people and the events of the Public Period of Christ around seven themes. We now organize the major events of this New Testament period around the last **seven days** in the life of Jesus.

Our four Gospel writers give various amounts of attention to each of these seven days. Notice in the following chart that Matthew and Mark each devote several chapters to Tuesday, whereas John does not even refer to it. On the other hand, John allocates five and a half chapters, approximately 25 percent of his entire book, to Thursday, compared to Matthew and Mark's half chapter each. Matthew and Luke both say something about all seven days.

As we examine more closely these seven days, we will use Luke's account (chapters 19–23) as our primary guide. In addition to writing about each of the seven days, he also writes chronologically. If, however, Luke omits something significant, we'll refer to one of the other writers which will allow us to ultimately merge all four accounts into one incredible story. By so doing, we will gain a deeper understanding and appreciation of what Jesus suffered during the Trials Period.

DAY	MATTHEW	MARK	LUKE	JOHN	NUMBER OF VERSES
Sunday	21:1–11, 14–17	11:1–11	19:28–44	12:12–19	53
Monday	21:12–13, 18–19	11:12–19	19:45–48	12:20–50	47
Tuesday	21:20–25:46	11:20–14:9	20:1–21:38		386
Wednesday	26:1–5, 14–16	14:1–2, 10–11	22:1–6		18
Thursday	26:17–75	14:12–72	22:7–65	13:1–18:27	182
Friday	27:1–61	15:1–47	22:66–23:56	18:28–19:42	225
Saturday	27:62–66		23:56		6

Christ's seven-day walk to the cross begins on a **Sunday**. He leaves Bethany and begins the two-mile trip to Jerusalem by walking west, up the Mount of Olives. Not long into this short trip, Jesus sends two of his disciples to Bethphage, a city located between Bethany and Jerusalem, to bring him a young donkey on which he rides for the remainder of the journey (Luke 19:29–35). Both Matthew and John remind their readers that by riding the young donkey Jesus fulfills the Old Testament messianic prophecy of Zechariah 9:9 that says, "Rejoice greatly, O daughter of Zion! Shout in triumph, O daughter of Jerusalem! Behold, your king is coming to you; He is just and endowed with salvation, humble, and mounted on a donkey, even on a colt, the foal of a donkey."

As Jesus rides the young donkey, the crowd begins to spread articles of clothing on the ground before him (Luke 19:36), which implies that they considered Jesus royalty (2 Kings 9:13). As if to erase any doubt of their esteem, they begin to praise him joyfully and loudly (Luke 19:37–38) by quoting from Psalm 118—a messianic psalm regularly sung during the Passover—saying, "Blessed is the King who comes in the name of the Lord." Two days later Jesus Himself will quote from this psalm.

As Christ begins his descent, He sees the city of Jerusalem and weeps (Luke 19:41–44) as He prophesies its future destruction, which the Romans fulfilled in AD 70. Upon entering the city Jesus goes to the temple, looks around (Mark 11:11), then departs with His twelve disciples to spend Sunday evening in Bethany. His **triumphal entry** into Jerusalem forces the Jewish rulers to act sooner than they wanted (Matthew 26:3–5), thus allowing Christ to be offered as the sacrificial lamb *on* Passover and not *after* Passover as they desired.

On **Monday** Jesus departs once again from Bethany, going over the Mount of Olives to Jerusalem. When He reaches the temple, He does more than just look around as He had done on the previous day. On this occasion he **cleanses the temple** (Luke 19:45–46), just as He had done at the beginning of His public ministry. As He casts out the people selling sacrificial animals and overturns the tables of the moneychangers, Jesus quotes from Isaiah 56:7, "My house shall be called a house of prayer for all the nations" and Jeremiah 7:11, "But you have made it a robbers' den" (Mark 11:17). By comprehending the meaning behind both of these verses, we can better appreciate why Jesus reacts so strongly.

When Solomon built the original temple, he designated the huge outer court as the court of the Gentiles (1 Kings 8:41–43, 59–60). Refer to the map of the temple on page 38. Though Gentiles could go no farther than the outer court, the Gentiles who came to Jerusalem to worship God during the Passover Feast at least had a place to worship (John 12:20). The presence of the sellers of the sacrificial animals and the moneychangers, however, makes less room for them.

On the one hand, Christ's righteous anger results partially from His desire for all the nations of the earth to have the opportunity to worship

God, thus prompting His quoting of Isaiah 56:7. On the other hand, Christ's response partially results from the motivation behind the selling of animals and changing of money. Worshipers traveling long distances could not always bring the necessary sacrificial animals which had to meet certain biblical standards. The synagogue officials responded by offering the pilgrims pre-approved animals for sacrifice but at a very high price. The moneychangers created a different racket but for the same greedy motive. The synagogue officials accepted only certain coinage in the temple. Someone coming from a different country would need to *buy* the correct kind of money in order to give an offering. Both the animal sellers and the moneychangers took advantage of the worshipers rather than serving them. This causes Jesus to compare them to the den of thieves found in Jeremiah 7:11.

After spending Monday night in Bethany, Jesus returns on **Tuesday** once again to the temple where the religious leaders confront him. We can best summarize day three as a day of **questions and answers**. The following chart organizes the questions asked, who asked them, and the answers given.

SCRIPTURE	PARTIES	QUESTION	ANSWER
Luke 20:1–18	Chief priests, scribes, and elders to Jesus	By what authority are You doing these things?	Answers their question with a question: Was the baptism of John from heaven or from men?
Luke 20:19–26	Pharisees, Herodians, scribes, and chief priests to Jesus	Is it lawful to pay taxes to Caesar, or not?	Render unto Caesar the things that are Caesar's, and to God the things that are God's.

Luke 20:27–38	Sadducees to Jesus	In the resurrection therefore, which wife will she be?	Those who are considered worthy to attain to that age . . . neither marry, nor are given in marriage.
Matt. 22:34–40	A lawyer from the party of the Pharisees to Jesus	Teacher, which is the great commandment in the Law?	You shall love the Lord your God with all your heart, and with all your soul, and with all your mind.
Luke 20:39–47	Jesus to the scribes	[If] David therefore calls [the Christ] Lord, how is He his son?	No one was able to answer Him a word. (Matt. 22:46)
Luke 21:1–36	The disciples—especially Peter, James, John, and Andrew—to Jesus (Mark 13:3)	When will these things be? (Matt. 24:3)	No one knows. (Matt. 24:36)
Luke 21:1–36	The disciples—especially Peter, James, John, and Andrew—to Jesus (Mark 13:3)	What will be the sign of Your coming and of the end of the age? (Matt. 24:3)	Tells of events before the end and events at the end. (Matt. 24:3–14, 15–31)

At the end of Tuesday, Jesus and his disciples retire to the Mount of Olives where they spend the night.

On **Wednesday,** Judas Iscariot, one of the Lord's inner circle, plots with the chief priests and officers how he might deliver Jesus over to them (Luke 22:1–6). In exchange for thirty pieces of silver (Matthew 26:15), **Judas agrees to betray Jesus** to them at a time when the multitude could not interfere. As to why Judas would betray Jesus after following Him for so long, we can only speculate. Regardless of the human motive, Scripture tells us that Satan's temptation ultimately causes Judas to negotiate the infamous deal (Luke 22:3).

During the day on **Thursday**, Jesus sends Peter and John to prepare the Passover meal for the Twelve and Himself (Luke 22:7–9) by purchasing the lamb, having it slain, and buying the other ingredients required for the ceremonial meal. As to the location of the meal, He gives them cryptic instructions. Rather than telling Peter and John the name of a family who volunteered to host the meal, he instructs them to look for a man carrying a pitcher of water (Luke 22:10) who, in turn, would show them a large upper room ready for them. The two disciples probably had no trouble finding their contact because typically only women and slaves performed such work. Keeping the location of the **Last Supper** a secret protects the group for a few more hours, providing the Lord critical time with His twelve disciples before Judas carries out his selfish betrayal.

That evening, Jesus and His disciples rendezvous at the upper room and begin to eat the Passover meal (Luke 22:14–18). At some point during the meal, the Son of God gets up from the table. After wrapping a towel around Himself, He begins to wash the feet of the Twelve, providing a powerful example of humility and servanthood (John 13:4–5).

Reclining once again at the table, Jesus becomes very troubled and announces that one of the group will betray him (Luke 22:21–23). In answer to John's question as to the betrayer's identity, Jesus hands a piece of food to Judas (John 13:25–26). Culturally, this action represents an offer of friendship, which could possibly mean Christ was offering Judas one last chance to change his mind about the betrayal. If so, it does not work, and Judas departs to carry out his diabolical plot.

With Judas gone Jesus takes the end of the meal in an unexpected direction (Luke 22:19–20). Holding some bread, Jesus gives thanks for it, breaks it, and then distributes it to the remaining disciples, as He declares, "This is My body which is given for you; do this in remembrance of Me." When the disciples finish eating the bread, the Lord takes one of the cups of wine from the table and once again, after giving thanks for it, gives it to the men to drink, saying, "This cup which is poured out for you is the new covenant in My blood." In an instant, Jesus infuses new meaning into a feast that the people of God had practiced for fifteen hundred years. The new celebration has come to be known as the Lord's Supper.

Amazingly, after or perhaps during the Passover meal the disciples begin arguing over who of them is the greatest (Luke 22:24–30). Jesus then predicts that Peter will deny Him three times before the rooster crows (Luke 22:31–34).

Jesus next gives detailed instructions to His disciples (John 14–17), stressing that though He would soon leave them, He would send his Holy Spirit to take His place. During this discourse Jesus and His disciples leave the upper room and cross the Kidron Valley to the Mount of Olives. They arrive about fifteen minutes later at a place called Gethsemane and enter a garden.

At the garden of **Gethsemane** (Luke 22:39), which means "olive press," Jesus instructs the majority of His disciples to sit while He goes to pray. Jesus, taking only Peter, James, and John, walks a stone's throw farther (Luke 22:41), where He tells the three that His soul grieves to the point of death. Leaving these three, the Lord goes a little farther, falls on His knees and face, and begins to ask God the Father, if possible, to remove the cup from Him. The cup refers to God's wrath toward the sin (Isaiah 51:17, 22) that Jesus would soon bear. The Lord dreads God's wrath so much that He sweats drops of blood (Luke 22:44), an extremely rare medical condition called hematidrosis in which great stress causes the surface capillaries to burst, releasing blood through pores in the skin.

Three times Christ fervently prays (Matthew 26:42, 44), asking if God could find any other way to restore the relationship between heaven and earth without Him suffering God's wrath. Each time, however, Jesus ends his prayer with His greater desire for God's will to be done.

The possible presence of the devil tempting Christ with an alternative to the cross may have added to His struggle. Earlier in the upper room, Jesus told the disciples (John 14:30) of the coming of the ruler of this world. The appearance of the angel to strengthen Jesus (Luke 22:43) brings to memory His wilderness experience. There, angels ministered to Jesus after the devil tempted Him and then departed for an opportune time (Matthew 4:11; Luke 4:13). The garden of Gethsemane may have been that opportune time.

GARDEN	Eden	Gethsemane
PERSON	Adam	Christ
CHOICE	Man's will	God's will
RESULT	Caused sin	Cured sin

Judas, about this time, accompanied by the chief priests, scribes, elders, officers of the temple, and perhaps as many as six hundred Roman soldiers to maintain order, arrives to betray Jesus (Luke 22:47–53; John 18:3). Because Jesus and the disciples have spent the last two nights on the Mount of Olives, Judas knows where he can find the Lord (John 18:2). In order to identify Jesus to the arresting officials, Judas kisses him, a practice used in that culture to demonstrate respect to a rabbi or teacher. Upon seeing the crowd, the disciples briefly resist but then flee for safety. Jesus, however, chooses to go peacefully.

Jesus spends the next several hours going through six trials, three of them religious and three of them civil. The first two religious trials occupy the remainder of Thursday night, whereas the final four trials occur early Friday morning. The Gospel of Luke mentions all but the first of these trials, which we find only in the Gospel of John. Let's briefly look at each of these trials.

From the garden of Gethsemane, the officials lead Jesus—with Peter and John following at a distance—bound to Annas (John 18:13–24) for the *first trial*. You may remember from the Private Period of Christ that Annas served as high priest from AD 6 to AD 15. Even though out of office and no longer officially serving as the high priest, he retains his influence and title, similar to that of a former president today. Annas questions Jesus about His disciples to see if he can find a way to charge Christ for inciting a revolution, and he asks Jesus about His teaching in an attempt to uncover anything blasphemous or heretical.

Next the officials lead Jesus to a different part of the palace where Caiaphas, the reigning high priest, and the Sanhedrin Council have assembled for the *second trial*. False witnesses stand ready because the court wants to obtain testimony against Jesus in order to put Him to death (Mark 14:55). Jesus remains silent. As dawn approaches, the trial increasingly proves a farce until Caiaphas does something that the law empowered only the high priest to do with an accused person. He places Jesus under oath by declaring, "I adjure You by the living God" (Matthew 26:63), and then he demands that Jesus tell the court whether He is the Christ (the Messiah), the Son of God. Answering affirmatively would signify equality with God, an offense punishable by death according to their law (Leviticus 24:16). Jesus answers, "I am" (Mark 14:62), a phrase recalling God's answer to Moses when he asked God for His name (Exodus 3:14). As if to underscore His answer, Jesus quotes from two messianic passages (Psalm 110:1; Daniel 7:13) and applies them to Himself. Considering His answer blasphemous, the Council concludes that Jesus deserves to die. Indeed, some on the Council immediately spit on Jesus and hit Him with their fists before the officers lead Him away into custody.

Early **Friday** morning (Luke 22:66) the guards take Jesus back before the Sanhedrin. The religious leaders now must hold a *third trial* and repeat their proceedings because they know that the previous trials had broken several laws both from Scripture and from their legal code: trying the accused at night, questioning the accused before witnesses spoke (John 18:21), and striking the accused before proving Him guilty (John 18:22).

Once again the leaders ask Jesus (Luke 22:70) if He is the Son of God. Once again He answers, "I am," and they condemn Him to death for blasphemy. They need the governor, however, to kill Jesus because the Roman occupiers restricted the Jews from executing anyone (John 18:31). This prohibition underscores God's providence in the sacrifice of His Son. Jews traditionally put people to death by stoning them, whereas the Romans used the cross. Jesus had long proclaimed (John 3:14; 12:32–33; 18:31–32) that He would die by crucifixion, thus fulfilling the Old Testament prophecies foretold in Psalm 22:16, Isaiah 53:5, and Zechariah 12:10.

As the religious officials lead Jesus to His next trial, Judas realizes he has set in motion the death of an innocent man. Feeling deeply remorseful, he returns the money—perhaps unaware that his actions fulfilled the Old Testament prophecy of Zechariah 11:12–13—and then departs to commit suicide by hanging himself.

TRIAL	AUTHORITY	OFFICIAL	OUTCOME
1 (John 18:13–24)	Religious (Jewish)	Annas	Finds nothing wrong that Jesus has done or said (John 18:23)
2 (Luke 22:54–65)	Religious (Jewish)	Caiaphas	Concludes Jesus has committed blasphemy (Mark 14:64)
3 (Luke 22:66–71)	Religious (Jewish)	Caiaphas	Concludes Jesus has committed blasphemy (Luke 22:70–71)
4 (Luke 23:1–5)	Civil (Roman)	Pontius Pilate	Finds no guilt in Jesus (Luke 23:4)
5 (Luke 23:6–12)	Civil (Roman)	Herod Antipas	Finds nothing wrong that Jesus has done or said (Luke 23:14, 15)
6 (Luke 23:13–25)	Civil (Roman)	Pontius Pilate	Finds no guilt in Jesus (Luke 23:14, 22; John 19:4, 6)

The religious officials lead Jesus from their chamber in the temple to the entrance of the Praetorium (John 18:28), the palace in which Pontius Pilate as the provincial governor resided when in the city. Caring more about outward appearances than inward holiness, the Jewish leaders hypocritically refuse to enter the Gentile Praetorium in order not to defile and disqualify themselves from participating in the Passover festivities. Not wanting to cause any unnecessary problems with the historically difficult leaders—especially in light of the large number of people who had gathered in the city during the week of Passover—Pilate walks outside to them and asks about their charge against Jesus, thus beginning Jesus' *fourth trial* (John 18:29).

Desiring a quick verdict, the religious officials distort the charge by repositioning Jesus from a religious blasphemer to a civil insurrectionist. They accuse Jesus (Luke 23:2) of three crimes: misleading the nation, forbidding the payment of taxes to Caesar, and claiming to be Christ, a king. In light of a revolutionary group known as the Zealots operating in Palestine at that time, Pilate understandably focuses on the accusation of Jesus claiming to be a king and summons Him to enter the Praetorium for questioning. Once inside, Pilate interrogates Jesus, asking if He claimed to be a king. Jesus answers affirmatively (Luke 23:3) but with a qualification. He explains that His kingdom is not of this world (John 18:36). Going back outside to the Jews, Pilate announces a verdict of innocence. Yet the crowd—consisting of the Sanhedrin, their servants, temple guards, and maybe some curious bystanders but not the general populace—insists on Jesus' guilt, clamoring that His teaching had agitated the people all across Judea, beginning with Galilee.

Upon learning that the accused came from Galilee, Pilate sees a way to calm the crowd and maintain the peace. He ignores the ruling he had just issued and defers the case to Herod Antipas, son of Herod the Great. Herod had arrived in Jerusalem to celebrate the Passover, and as tetrarch of Galilee, he had legal jurisdiction over disputes occurring in that district.

Having Jesus appear before him pleases Herod Antipas because he had long heard about Jesus and wanted to see Him perform one of His famous miracles. During this *fifth trial* (Luke 23:8–12) the chief priests and the scribes vehemently accuse Jesus while Herod Antipas, the one who had John the Baptist beheaded, questions Him at length. Jesus does not speak, and Herod shrewdly declines to issue a potentially unpopular verdict. He and his soldiers mock and mistreat the Lord before dressing Jesus in a beautiful robe and sending Him back to Pilate.

Back at the Praetorium, Pilate begins the *sixth trial* by stating to the religious officials that neither he nor Herod Antipas had found Jesus guilty of the charges (Luke 23:14, 15). In order to placate the crowd without giving in to their demands, Pilate offers to release a Jewish prisoner, an annual practice of his during the Passover. He gives the crowd the choice of Jesus or Barabbas, who was a true insurrectionist, a known robber, and a notorious murderer (Luke 23:19; John 18:40).

When the crowd chooses Barabbas, Pilate tries a different tact to satisfy the bloodthirsty Jews. He tells them that he will punish Jesus and then release Him. As punishment Pilate decides to whip Jesus. Do not, however, confuse this particular beating with the more brutal scourging that occurs a bit later in the morning. Pilate permits this punishment in hope of gaining Jesus' release by appealing to the sympathies of the Jews. Though severe, the pain of this whipping pales when compared to the pain of the latter scourging. After the beating the soldiers place a crown of thorns on Jesus' head and drape Him in a purple robe, all the while mocking Him as a king and hitting Him in the face (Luke 23:16; John 19:1–3).

Wanting to preserve Roman justice by releasing the innocent man, Pilate goes back outside the Praetorium and once again addresses the religious officials (Luke 23:20), telling them that he had found no guilt in the accused (John 19:4). He presents the bloodied Jesus (John 19:5), wearing a robe and crown with the words, "Behold the man!" as if to declare that certainly this pathetic figure could not be a king. Incredibly, the crowd persists in its cry for death, calling for Pilate to crucify Jesus (Luke 23:21; John 19:6). As Pilate continues to resist their demand, pointing once again to the fact of Jesus' innocence (Luke 23:22; John 19:6), the Jews reveal their true issue. They want Jesus put to death because He claimed to be the Son of God (John 19:7), a crime calling for death according to their Jewish law.

Hearing that Jesus claimed deity, Pilate takes Jesus back inside the Praetorium to question Him about his origin (John 19:8, 9). After interrogating Jesus and perhaps remembering the warning from his wife (Matthew 27:19), Pilate returns outside to the religious officials and once again makes an effort to release Jesus (John 19:12).

The religious officials then threaten Pilate: if he releases Jesus, they will seek to prove he had committed treason against the Roman emperor, Caesar Tiberius. Their threatened testimony that Pilate supported a revolutionary could lead to the loss of his position or even his life.

PILATE DECLARES JESUS INNOCENT

1st Time	Luke 23:4	John 18:38
2nd Time	Luke 23:14, 15	
3rd Time		John 19:4
4th Time	Luke 23:22	John 19:6

As Pilate considers his options—executing an innocent man but restoring peace versus preserving justice but possibly losing his position—a riot begins (Matthew 27:24). Washing his hands as though to cleanse himself of any guilt, Pilate grants the crowd's demand (Luke 23:24) and pronounces the sentence: death by crucifixion (Mark 15:15; John 19:16). Typical for that day, Pilate first has a soldier scourge Jesus by tying Him to a post and then lashing His back with a whip made of leather thongs containing sharp pieces of metal and bone. Jews limited a scourging to thirty-nine lashes for fear of accidentally violating the law found in Deuteronomy 25:3. A Roman scourging, however, continued until the soldier grew tired. Jesus experiences a Roman scourging that leaves strips of flesh hanging from his body. Jesus, unlike most people, survives the scourging. After further mocking and mistreatment by the soldiers, they lead Him away to his crucifixion.

History provides abundant information about the gruesome procedure of a Roman **crucifixion** (Luke 23:33), a form of execution developed in order to prolong the person's life while maximizing the amount of pain experienced. In fact, a crucifixion caused so much pain that a new word arose, one from which we get the word *excruciating*, meaning "from or out of the crucifixion."

At approximately 9 A.M. (Mark 15:25), probably four soldiers (John 19:23) begin their task by stripping Jesus of all his clothes and placing His raw, bloody back on the rough wood of the crossbeam that, at this point, remained flat on the ground. Careful not to break Jesus' bones or pierce major blood vessels, the soldiers nail approximately six-inch-long spikes through each of Christ's wrists rather than His palms, because the hand muscle cannot long support a writhing victim's weight. After accomplishing this painful act, the soldiers lift the crossbeam and attach it to a vertical post (probably not as tall as most pictures show) permanently planted in the ground. Next, the executioners nail a spike between the bones of Jesus' feet. As they do so, they take great care to ensure His legs remain bent at the knees. Bent knees would allow Jesus to pull up on His nail-pierced wrists to release the tension in His torso and enable Him to breathe. Bending the knees in no way demonstrated mercy. Just the opposite. It maliciously keeps Jesus alive longer and thus exposes Him to more pain. Depending on the severity of the scourging, a person could survive on the cross in agony for days. Yet in spite of the intense agony, Jesus prays, "Father, forgive them; for they do not know what they are doing" (Luke 23:34).

Before finishing their duty, the soldiers fasten the sign bearing Jesus' name and crime to the top of the cross: "Jesus the Nazarene, the King of the Jews" (Luke 23:38; John 19:19). Their task now complete, the four soldiers gamble for the robe and other articles of Christ's clothing (John 19:23, 24), not realizing that by doing so they were fulfilling another Old Testament prophecy found in Psalm 22:18.

Soon the religious officials, soldiers, and others begin to mock Jesus (Luke 23:36–37). Even one of the two criminals crucified beside Jesus mocks Him. The other criminal, however, declares Jesus as innocent and asks the Messiah to remember him in the future, to which Jesus answers, "Truly I say to you, today you shall be with Me in Paradise" (Luke 23:39–43). Also in the crowd stand some of Jesus' followers. Conspicuously absent are the men, probably choosing to remain out of sight due to fear of the Jewish leaders. John alone witnesses the death of his Lord. Presumably, his young age eliminates him as a threat. After addressing the criminal beside Him, Jesus instructs John to care for His mother (John 19:25–27).

CHRIST'S SEVEN LAST STATEMENTS ON THE CROSS

1 (Luke 23:34)	"Father, forgive them; for they do not know what they are doing."
2 (Luke 23:43)	"Truly I say to you, today you shall be with Me in Paradise."
3 (John 19:26, 27)	"Woman, behold, your son!" "Behold, your mother!"
4 (Mark 15:34)	"My God, My God, why hast Thou forsaken Me?"
5 (John 19:28)	"I am thirsty."
6 (John 19:30)	"It is finished!"
7 (Luke 23:46)	"Father, into Thy hands I commit My spirit."

At approximately noon the sky grows dark and remains that way until 3 P.M. (Luke 23:44). Scripture remains quiet about what happens during these three hours. At 3 P.M., however, Jesus loudly quotes the first verse of Psalm 22, "My God, My God, why hast Thou forsaken Me?" (Mark 15:34). In Jesus' day, people did not number the psalms as we do today, so the Jews identified each psalm by its first verse. That means that a teacher wanting students to read Psalm 23 would direct them to turn to "The Lord is my shepherd," causing the rest of the psalm's verses to flood the minds of those hearing. With that understanding, consider what the crowd must have thought when they heard, "My God, My God, why hast Thou forsaken Me?" The chart below highlights some of the verses in Psalm 22 and compares them to the scene unfolding before the followers of Jesus as they witnessed His crucifixion. As you read the psalm, you'll see even more similarities.

PSALM 22	CHRIST'S CRUCIFIXION
"My God, my God, why hast Thou forsaken Me?" (v. 1)	"My God, My God, why hast Thou forsaken Me?" (Matt. 27:46)
"For there is none to help." (v. 11)	"Then all the disciples left Him and fled." (Matt. 26:56)
"And my tongue cleaves to my jaws." (v. 15)	"I am thirsty." (John 19:28)
"They pierced my hands and my feet." (v. 16)	"And when they had crucified Him . . ." (Matt. 27:35)
"They divide my garments among them, and for my clothing they cast lots." (v. 18)	"They divided up His garments among themselves, casting lots." (Matt. 27:35)

Around 3 P.M. (Matthew 27:46), Jesus, recognizing that He has accomplished His mission and will soon die, utters that He thirsts (John

19:28). Someone moistens His mouth with sour wine, using a hyssop branch (reminding us of Exodus 12:21–23) to reach Him (John 19:29). Though some in the crowd did not understand His comment regarding His thirst, with His mouth now moistened, everyone clearly hears and understands His next two sentences.

First, He victoriously proclaims, "It is finished!" (John 19:30)—a phrase merchants declared when someone paid a debt in full—signifying that by His death He had paid in full the penalty for humanity's disobedience to God. Isaiah had prophesied, "But He was pierced through for our transgressions, He was crushed for our iniquities; the chastening for our well-being fell upon Him, and by His scourging we are healed. All of us like sheep have gone astray, each of us has turned to his own way; but the Lord has caused the iniquity of us all to fall on Him" (Isaiah 53:5–6).

Second, just before breathing His last breath, Jesus loudly quotes Psalm 31:5, "Father, into Thy hands I commit My spirit," (Luke 23:46) a psalm the Jews in that day often recited as an evening prayer.

At the moment of Jesus' death several strange events occur as though to verify the Messiah's identity. An earthquake takes place. The thick veil in the temple that separated the Holy of Holies from the rest of the temple rips from top to bottom, powerfully signifying that everyone—not just the high priest once a year on the Day of Atonement—may now enter the presence of God through the death of the ultimate Passover Lamb (see Hebrews 9). Additionally, many followers of Christ who previously had died come back to life (Matthew 27:51–53). Interestingly, approximately thirty minutes earlier, the priests offered the Passover lambs in the temple.

At some point during the day, the Jewish rulers ask Pilate to break the legs of the three men hanging on the crosses (John 19:31). Deuteronomy 21:22–23 explains why they made this seemingly strange request. The Jewish law demanded that the bodies not hang on the "trees" overnight so the land would not be defiled. With the important Passover Sabbath beginning that evening, the Jews want the bodies removed sooner rather than later. Breaking the lower legs of someone hanging on a cross would hasten death. Without the support of his legs, a man's entire weight would pull down on his chest muscles, restricting his ability to inhale and causing asphyxiation.

As the soldiers approach Jesus to break His legs, they realize He is dead. Perhaps to make sure, one of them stabs Him in the side with a spear (John 19:32–34). When the apostle John writes about the event years later, he notes how the soldiers fulfill two Old Testament prophecies: Psalm 34:20, "Not a bone of Him shall be broken"; and Psalm 22:16, "They pierced my hands and my feet." David's prophecies become all the more amazing when we realize that (1) he penned his words during a time when the Israelites used stoning to execute condemned people, and (2) he made his prediction hundreds of years before the Romans introduced crucifixion as their form of capital punishment.

That evening, a follower of Jesus by the name of Joseph, who also served in the Sanhedrin, courageously asks Pilate if he may bury the Lord's body (Luke 23:50–55). Normally, the Romans would simply throw the body in the garbage dump outside the city, because condemned criminals lost the right to a proper burial. After receiving permission, Joseph—who lived in Arimathea, a town twenty miles northwest of Jerusalem—takes the body of Jesus down from the cross with the help of Nicodemus. This act of devotion means even more when we remember that according to Jewish law, touching a dead body defiled them and, as a result, disqualified them from participating in the Passover.

Followed by John, Mary the mother of Jesus, and other women from Galilee (Mark 15:47), Joseph and Nicodemus take the body of Jesus to Joseph's own nearby tomb, which had recently been carved into the rock (see Isaiah 53:9). After washing the body according to the Jewish custom, they wrap the Messiah in a linen cloth filled with spices and bury him (John 19:39–41). Before leaving the burial place, Joseph rolls a large dish-shaped stone, probably close to three feet in diameter, in front of the entrance of the tomb (Matthew 27:60).

TRIALS PERIOD

DAY	MAJOR EVENT
Sunday	Triumphal entry
Monday	Cleansing of temple
Tuesday	Questions and answers
Wednesday	Judas's plot
Thursday	Last Supper and Gethsemane
Friday	Crucifixion
Saturday	Guards put at tomb

On the next day, **Saturday** (Luke 23:56), the chief priests and the Pharisees arrange a meeting with Pilate, the result of which ultimately provides powerful evidence for Christ's resurrection. Fearing that the followers of Jesus might steal His body and afterward announce His resurrection from the dead, they ask Pilate to protect the tomb from the threat of theft. Pilate grants them a guard, according to some researchers, of four **Roman soldiers**. He instructs the Jewish leaders to make the tomb as secure as possible. Part of their effort includes setting a Roman seal on the stone. This precaution probably involves stretching a cord across the stone and holding it in place with clay or wax, all to detect any tampering with the stone. The seal represents to any who dared go near the grave that the great power of Rome guards the entrance.

With the cross stained with blood, the long awaited Messiah dead, the grave sealed, the disciples scattered, and all hope lost, the Trials Period of Christ ends in despair. Yet in just a few short hours all that would change. But for now let's look at where the events of these seven days occur.

WHERE?

The following maps orient us to the geographical locations of these events. Though Nazareth and Capernaum are the major cities of the Private and Public Periods of Christ's life, **Jerusalem** clearly stands as the center of activity for His Trials Period. We can catalog the events of Sunday through Wednesday by drawing a mental east-west line from Bethany over the Mount of Olives to the temple in Jerusalem. For three days Jesus moves back and forth along this line. He leaves Sunday morning from the town of Bethany (1) and walks west, stopping in Bethphage (2) for the young colt. He continues His journey by crossing the Mount of Olives (3) before arriving in Jerusalem for His triumphal entry. Later in the day on Sunday, the Lord retraces His steps to Bethany. On Monday Jesus journeys the exact same path and cleanses the temple (4) before returning again to Bethany. Tuesday's trip repeats the two miles (John 11:18) to Jerusalem along the same road, and on this day the Lord answers the questions of various groups. Jesus spends Tuesday night in an enclosure called the garden of Gethsemane (5), located on the west side of the Mount of Olives. Jesus possibly spends Wednesday and Wednesday night in this same garden.

Christ's Trials Period
(Sunday — Wednesday)

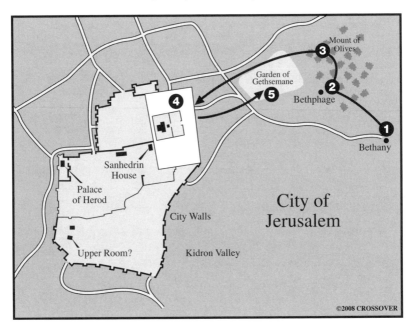

On Thursday, Jesus leaves the garden of Gethsemane (5) and enters Jerusalem, proceeding to a prearranged home. Entering its upper room (6), He participates in the Passover meal with His disciples. Many scholars suspect that the home belonged to John Mark's parents and that possibly other key meetings (Acts 1:13; 12:12) occur there. From this upper room they return to the garden of Gethsemane where Judas arrives to betray Jesus.

From the garden the religious rulers take the Lord to the house of the high priest (7) where Jesus endures the first two religious trials. At daylight on Friday morning the Jewish authorities take Him to the temple (8) for the third religious trial. From there they lead Jesus to the Praetorium (9) where He stands trial before Pilate who then sends Jesus to Herod's palace (10) for his judgment. Choosing not to cast a verdict, Herod returns Jesus to the Praetorium.

Christ's Trials Period
(Thursday – Saturday)

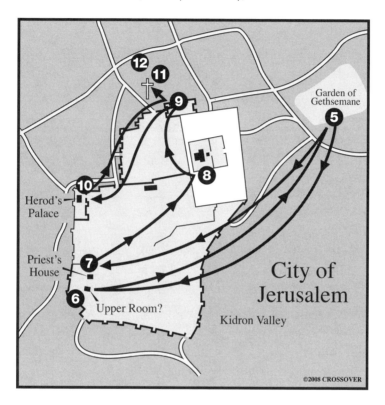

When Pilate finally reaches a verdict, the Roman soldiers march Jesus to Golgotha (11) for the crucifixion. After Jesus' death, Joseph and Nicodemus carry the body of the Messiah to a nearby tomb (12).

Now that we have a better understanding about where each of the key events occurred, let's look more closely at the timing of it all.

WHEN?

Because the Trials Period of Christ lasts for only **one week**, you might think it an easy task to determine which events occurred on which day of the week. Not so. Actually it can get a bit confusing, because not one of the Gospel writers notes when all seven days begin and end. To determine the specific day each activity happened takes a bit of investigation. Fortunately, the Gospel writers provide the necessary clues.

Take a few minutes, using the Scriptures provided below, to fill in the following chart which harmonizes the verses in chronological order. After reading the scriptural references, note in the Day column which day you think the verses address, and in the Clue column note the evidence that supports your decision. By so doing, you'll construct for yourself a simple timeline. To get you started, read John 12:1–11. Remember from the previous chapter that the Passover fell on Friday during the year of Christ's crucifixion. So John 12:1–11 discusses the events on Saturday. Now continue with 12:12–15 in the chart below. The passages without parentheses are the key sources in the chronology.

MATTHEW	MARK	LUKE	JOHN	CLUE	DAY	EVENT
			12:12–15	John 12:12 "The next day"	Sunday	Triumphal entry
	11:7–18			Mark 11:12		Cleansing of temple
(26:2)	11:19–20			Mark 11:20		Questions and answers
		20:1–22:6		Luke 21:37–38		Judas's plot
(26:17)	(14:12)	22:7–20	(13:1)	Luke 22:7		Last Supper and Gethsemane
(27:1)	(15:1)	22:54–23:1		Luke 22:66		Crucifixion
27:50–66		(23:56)		Matthew 27:62		Guards put at tomb

PUTTING TOGETHER THE PUZZLE OF THE NEW TESTAMENT

Now use the above chart and the chart on page 91 to note in your Bible when each day begins. Do this exercise by writing in the margins of Matthew, Mark, Luke, and John the start of each of the last seven days in the life of Christ. In the future when you reread the Gospels in your Bible, you'll remember the day of the week the event took place and, as a result, have a better understanding of its chronological context.

At this point we understand much more about how, where, and when the Messiah died on the cross, yet a much more important question needs answering.

WHY?

Recall once again the overall theme of the Bible: **God receiving glory by restoring fellowship between the nations and Himself through His Son, Jesus Christ**. God solved the problem of breaking either His law or His heart by sending His Son, Jesus Christ, to pay the penalty of man's disobedience by dying in man's place (2 Corinthians 5:21). As a result of the Messiah's substitutionary atonement, every person everywhere now has access to fellowship with God. Receiving this wonderful blessing requires nothing more or less than believing that Jesus' work on the cross makes you right with God.

During this Trials Period, even as the pain of the cross should have preoccupied His attention, Christ's desire for all people groups to experience this glorious fellowship with God manifested itself. On Monday Jesus cleanses the court of the *Gentiles* in the temple by expelling those selling sacrificial animals and changing money. As He does this He quotes Isaiah 56:7, "My house will be called a house of prayer for *all nations*" (Mark 11:17 TNIV). Later that day, when Philip and Andrew bring some *Greeks* to Jesus, He tells them if lifted up, He will draw *all men* to Himself (John 12:32). To the multitude He proclaims that He came to save *the world* (John 12:47).

On Tuesday, when his disciples ask about the end of the age, Jesus responds that first the gospel will be preached in the *whole world* as a witness to *all the nations* (Matthew 24:3, 14). Referring to the coming judgment, he stresses that believers will come from *all the nations* (Matthew 25:32). Interestingly, on Friday only moments after the death of Christ, a Gentile—the Roman centurion in charge of the crucifixion—seems to be the first person after the crucifixion to proclaim Jesus as the Son of God (Matthew 27:54).

So why did Jesus go to the cross to be slain as the ultimate Passover Lamb? He did so in order to make fellowship with Holy God accessible by faith to all nations so that not only Jews but also Greeks, Romans, and even the whole world could glorify God.

Let's now take a look at a third author in the New Testament to see what we can learn about him.

WHO?

Since Luke wrote 20 percent of the chapters in the New Testament, it may surprise you to discover that only three verses mention him by name: Colossians 4:14; 2 Timothy 4:11; and Philemon 24. Yet in spite of such a paucity of references, we can learn quite a bit about the author of two of the longest books in the New Testament: the Gospel according to Luke and the Acts of the Apostles, otherwise known as the books of Luke and Acts.

THE WRITINGS OF LUKE

Luke	Details the Coming of Christ Era
Acts	Details the Going of the Church Era

We can make four observations about Luke. First, from Colossians 4:14 we know Luke works as a medical doctor, and we can assume he uses his training to mend Paul's wounds after his beating for delivering the Philippian slave girl from the spirit of divination (Acts 16:22–24). Second, from a passage in Colossians we know that Luke is Gentile and not Jewish. As Paul closes his letter to the Colossians (4:10–11), he sends them greetings from three of his companions: Aristarchus, Mark (Barnabas' cousin), and Justus. All three of these Paul describes as the only fellow workers with him from the circumcision, in other words, Jewish. Paul then highlights other companions presumably not from the circumcision and includes Luke (Colossians 4:12–14). We find another clue that supports our belief that Luke is Gentile from Acts 1:19. In this verse Luke makes a revealing comment describing Aramaic—the Hebrew dialect spoken during New Testament times by the Jewish people—as "their" language.

Philemon 24 allows us to make a third observation about Luke. This Gentile physician serves as a fellow worker with the apostle Paul. A number of other passages allow us to conclude that Luke serves in this capacity for many years. If you carefully read the book of Acts, you'll notice that in three places Luke changes from third person plural (they) to first person plural (we), indicating Luke's presence during some of the events he describes (Acts 16:10–17; 20:5–21; 27:1–28:16). As we will see later, a couple of years after Paul's release from house arrest, the Romans throw Paul in prison again and finally execute him. During this last imprisonment, Paul wrote 2 Timothy. In this letter, Paul states that only Luke remains with him. Putting the bits and pieces together, we see that Luke co-labors with Paul from Paul's second missionary journey until Paul's death.

Finally, we observe that Luke writes his two-volume series from the perspective of a historian. The recipient of his work was Theophilus (Luke 1:3; Acts 1:1). This name, which means either "lover of god" or "loved by god," probably did not represent a real *name* in order to protect the recipient. "Theophilus" probably did, however, represent an actual *person,* because Luke calls him "most excellent," a title reserved for people of high rank in Roman society (Acts 24:2–3; 26:25). In the introduction to his gospel (1:1–4), Luke explains to Theophilus that, because he wants Theophilus to know the exact truth about the things of Christ, he (Luke) investigated everything carefully and laid out his findings in consecutive order. Luke also shows this attention to historical detail in passages such as Luke 2:1–2 about the birth of Christ and Luke 3:1–2 about the beginning of John the Baptist's ministry.

FOR NEXT TIME

If you are having an extremely busy week:	If you have a little extra time:	If you can't get enough:
read John 20–21.	add Matthew 28, Mark 16, and Luke 24.	add 1 John, 2 John, and 3 John.

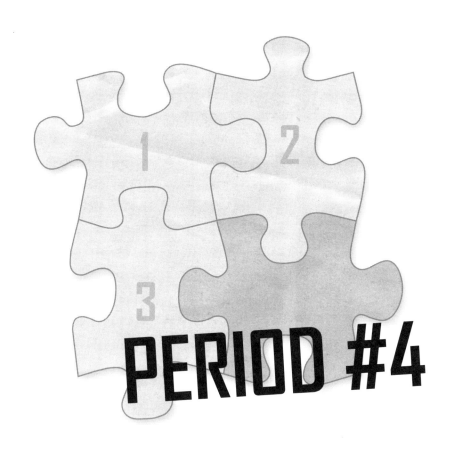

PERIOD #4

PERIOD #4

Christ's Triumphant Period

Though the previous chapter covers only seven days in the life of Christ, it contains many details. If we don't diligently review the two eras and eight periods of the New Testament, we can lose sight of how the specifics relate to the overall picture. On the other hand, if we regularly remind ourselves of what we've learned, then the content will become part of our long-term memory. So let's make the effort once again to complete the following chart.

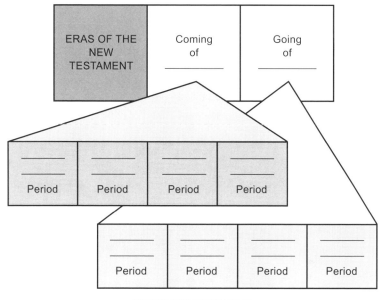

At this point in our adventure we've identified twenty-one key items that summarize the New Testament events found in the first three periods of the Coming of Christ Era: seven groups of people; seven themes during Christ's public ministry; and, in the previous chapter, the last seven days of Christ's life. Mastering these twenty-one key items allows us to communicate New Testament history in a chronological order that others will find thorough yet simple enough to remember. Place the key items in the chart below. If the third column confuses you, refer to the Trials Period chart found on page 91 of chapter three.

PERIOD #1 SEVEN GROUPS	PERIOD #2 SEVEN THEMES	PERIOD #3 SEVEN DAYS
Born to_____ and _____	Inspires the _____	_____ occurs on Sunday
Worshiped by_____	Instructs the _____	_____occurs on Monday
Honored by _____ and _____	Infuriates the _____	_____ occurs on Tuesday
Sought by _____ and _____	Causes _____	_____ occurs on Wednesday
Taught by temple_____	Cures the _____	_____ and _____ occur on Thursday
Baptized by_____	Casts out _____	_____ occurs on Friday
Tempted by_____	Reveals that we can be _____	_____ occurs on Saturday

The previous chapter, the Trials Period of Christ, ended with the followers of Christ discouraged and defeated. The Lord Jesus no longer lives but lies buried in a tomb guarded by Roman soldiers. Yet events soon unfold that will radically alter not only everybody's perspective but also the course of history. As Sunday morning's dawn races toward Jerusalem's horizon, the Trials Period of Christ abruptly comes to a close and the Triumphant Period of Christ breaks forth on all mankind. Let's see what happens.

WHAT?

At the end of the Trials Period, the Lord Jesus pays the penalty of humanity's sin by shedding His blood. Yet how can we know with certainty that the death of Jesus propitiates, or satisfies, God's anger toward our disobedience? In 1 Corinthians 15:17 we learn that "if Christ has not been raised, your faith is worthless; you are still in your sins." God raised Christ from the dead to reveal that He had accepted Christ's work of redemption on the cross. This event occurs in what we call the Triumphant Period of Christ. This fourth and final period of the Coming of Christ Era stresses **the presentation of the Messiah.** Each of the Gospel writers devotes his last chapter or chapters to this glorious time.

CHRIST'S TRIUMPHANT PERIOD

Matthew	Mark	Luke	John
1 chapter	1 chapter	1 chapter	2 chapters
(28:1–20)	(16:1–20)	(24:1–53)	(20:1–21:25)

If the Private and Public periods give an extended introduction to the seven days of the Trials Period, then the Triumphant Period provides a powerful conclusion to the most wonderful story ever told.

Let's examine closely how God the Father performs this amazing miracle of miracles, assuring the restoration of fellowship between Himself and people of all times and places who receive by faith the gift of His Son, the Messiah, whom we know as Jesus Christ the Lord.

HOW?

We can crystallize the events in this final action-packed period of the Coming of Christ Era by noting **three confidence builders**: Christ's empty tomb, appearances, and ascension. Let's look at the first confidence builder, the empty tomb.

The Gospel writers devote a total of forty-three verses to **the empty tomb**. Let's take the verses in the chart below and harmonize them into one story. We'll use John's Gospel as our primary source, because of the four authors he presents the only eyewitness record to all three of the confidence builders and devotes twice as many chapters to this period as the others. Yet as we found in the previous periods, we cannot obtain the full picture of what happens during this time frame without referring to the accounts of the other Gospel writers.

CONFIDENCE BUILDER #1

THE EMPTY TOMB

Matthew 28:1–8, 11–15	Mark 16:1–8	Luke 24:1–12	John 20:1–10

We pick up the story early Sunday morning before daylight. At some point during the darkness several incredible events take place—primarily Jesus rises from the dead. An earthquake also occurs as an angel descends from heaven, rolls away the large stone blocking the entrance to Jesus' tomb, and sits down on top of it (Matthew 28:2). Keep in mind that the angel removes the stone not to let Jesus out, but to let the world see that Christ had indeed risen from the dead! The angel's overwhelming appearance causes the soldiers to faint (Matthew 28:3–4). Upon recovering, they go into the city and tell the chief priests what had happened. The chief priests bribe the soldiers to say that the disciples stole the body of Jesus while the soldiers slept (Matthew 28:11–15).

Just before dawn, Mary Magdalene arrives at the grave site (John 20:1). At daybreak, other women—Mary the mother of James, Salome, Joanna the wife of Chuza the steward of Herod (Luke 8:3), and at least one other unnamed woman (Mark 16:1; Luke 24:10)—join Mary Magdalene at the tomb to anoint the body of Jesus with spices, an act both of devotion and necessity. In that culture, the Jews anointed dead bodies with spices to help eliminate the pungent order of decaying flesh. Seeing that someone had removed the stone from the entrance to the tomb, the women look inside (Luke 24:3). Instead of finding the body of Jesus, they discover two angels dressed in dazzling white apparel (Mark 16:5; Luke 24:4). One of the angels announces that Jesus the Nazarene had risen from the dead (Matthew 28:5–6; Mark 16:6; Luke 24:5–7). The angel then instructs them to go tell His disciples that He will meet them in Galilee (Matthew 28:7; Mark 16:7).

Trembling with fear and great joy, the women run and report this marvelous encounter both to the eleven disciples and to other followers of Christ (John 20:2; Luke 24:9). Though most of the apostles consider the talk nonsense (Luke 24:11), Peter and John run to the tomb, with John arriving first (John 20:3–4). Peering inside, John does not see the body of Jesus or the angels. He sees only the linen wrappings in the place where Jesus had been lain. When Peter arrives they both go inside the tomb (John 20:5–8). After investigating the evidence of the linen wrapping and the neatly arranged face cloth, the two of them leave the tomb (John 20:10).

If these first two trips to Jesus' tomb alarmed the visitors, then the next trip to the tomb amazes them. The living Lord Jesus reveals Himself, proving that no one had stolen the body, as the soldiers might testify, but that He had risen from the dead. For the next forty days Jesus the Messiah makes ten recorded **appearances** to His followers.

After telling about their experience, *perhaps* Mary Magdalene and the other women return to the tomb. Who wouldn't want to return to the tomb if only to see the angels again? (Please note the word *perhaps* in the first sentence. Scholars disagree as to the exact order of the events on Sunday morning. Though the following suggested arrangement harmonizes the Scripture, it is presented with great humility. This timeline represents only one perspective.) If they do return to the tomb—as this section of Scripture coupled with a later conversation between two disciples and Jesus seems to indicate (Luke 24:22–24)—then by the time the women arrive Peter and John have already left the tomb.

It appears that Mary Magdalene reaches the tomb before the other women. Whether she ran ahead or left earlier, we don't know. After weeping outside the tomb Mary Magdalene looks inside (John 20:11) and sees the two angels sitting where Joseph of Arimathea and Nicodemus previously had laid the body of Jesus (John 20:12–13). As she turns around she finds someone else present, the risen Lord Jesus (John 20:14–16; Mark 16:9). Overjoyed, Mary Magdalene begins to cling to Him (John 20:17). At some point, the other women arrive. Coming up to Jesus, they bow to the ground, take hold of His feet, and begin to worship Him (Matthew 28:9). Returning to the disciples, Mary Magdalene reports that she had seen Jesus alive (John 20:18; Mark 16:10), but they refuse to believe her (Mark 16:11).

The next appearance occurs later that day as Cleopas and another unnamed disciple of Jesus walk from Jerusalem to Emmaus, a small town about seven miles away. They apparently had heard the reports of the empty tomb from Mary and the women as well as from Peter and John, but they seem to have left the city before hearing the women's report of their second trip to the tomb in which the women actually met the living Lord Jesus (Luke 24:22–24). Somewhere along the journey Jesus joins the two travelers. Like Mary Magdalene (John 20:15), they do not initially recognize Him (Luke 24:13–16). Along the way Jesus explains from the Old Testament why the Christ had to suffer (Luke 24:25–27). Arriving at Emmaus, the men invite Jesus to join them for a meal because evening would soon arrive. As Jesus blesses the bread, He allows the two disciples to recognize Him but immediately vanishes from their sight (Luke 24:28–32).

Awed at seeing the living Lord Jesus, the two disciples quickly return to Jerusalem and find all the apostles, with the exception of Thomas, gathered together in one room (Luke 24:33). Before they can relate their amazing experience (Luke 24:35), the Eleven announce that the risen Lord Jesus had appeared to Peter (Luke 24:34).

While the two from Emmaus relate to the apostles their encounter with the risen Lord, Jesus suddenly appears among them (Luke 24:36–37). This fifth appearance no doubt startles and frightens His followers (Luke 24:37) because He enters the room in spite of shut doors (John 20:19). Because they considered Him a ghost, Jesus shows them the wounds in His hands, feet, and side (Luke 24:39; John 20:20). Imagine the moment! When the disciples tell Thomas they had seen the living Lord, Thomas announces that unless he put his finger in the place of the nails and his hand into Jesus' side, he would not believe it (perhaps because of Jesus' words in Matthew 24:23: "Then if anyone says to you, 'Behold, here is the Christ,' or 'There He is,' do not believe him").

Eight days later Jesus once again appears as the disciples meet behind closed doors (John 20:26). This time He focuses on Thomas, command-ing him to touch His hands and side. Upon seeing the risen Lord, Thomas proclaims Jesus as his Lord and God (John 20:27–28).

Sometime after this appearance to the Eleven (John 21:1), they travel to Galilee as Jesus had instructed them on the first day of His resurrection. Once there, Peter decides to go fishing one night, and six of the disciples join him (John 21:2–3). They catch nothing. As the day dawns, they can see and hear a man on the beach, but they don't recognize him (John 21:4–5). At the man's suggestion, they cast the net on the right-hand side of the boat and catch so many fish they cannot haul them into the boat (John 21:6). When John tells Peter that he recognizes the man on the beach as Jesus, Peter dives into the water and swims to shore (John 21:7). Once everyone arrives, they eat a breakfast prepared for them by the Lord (John 21:8–14). Afterward, Jesus takes Peter aside and instructs him to care for His sheep (John 21:15–23).

CONFIDENCE BUILDER #2

THE APPEARANCES

APPEARANCES	WITNESSES	DAY	SCRIPTURE
1	Mary Magdalene at the tomb	1	Mark 16:9–11; John 20:11–18
2	The women (Mary mother of James, Salome, Joanna, and at least one other)	1	Matthew 28:9–10
3	Cleopas and an unnamed disciple on the road to Emmaus	1	Mark 16:12–13; Luke 24:13–32
4	Peter in Jerusalem	1	Luke 24:33–35; 1 Corinthians 15:5
5	Ten of the apostles in Jerusalem; Thomas absent	1	Mark 16:14; Luke 24:36–43; John 20:19–25
6	Eleven of the apostles, especially Thomas, in Jerusalem	9	John 20:26–31;1 Corinthians 15:5
7	Peter, Thomas, Nathanael, James, John, and two others while fishing in Galilee	Between days 13 and 38	John 21:1–25
8	The eleven apostles at a mountain in Galilee (maybe with more than five hundred of His followers)	Between days 13 and 38	Matthew 28:16–20; Mark 16:15–18; 1 Corinthians 15:6
9	James, the half-brother of Jesus	?	1 Corinthians 15:7
10	The disciples in Jerusalem	40	Luke 24:44–49; Acts 1:3–8

Before discussing the next recorded appearance of the risen Lord Jesus, think back to the very first visit to the empty tomb. Do you recall what the angel instructed the women to tell the disciples? Matthew 28:7 puts it this way, "And go quickly and tell His disciples that He has risen from the dead; and behold, He is going before you into Galilee, there you will see Him; behold, I have told you." The eighth appearance probably refers to this rendezvous. The Eleven arrive at a mountain previously designated by Jesus, and He reveals Himself to them (Matthew 28:16–17). At the mountain Jesus mandates that His followers go and make disciples of all the nations, baptizing them and teaching them to observe all that He commanded.

We assume that the five hundred or more followers who see the Lord in 1 Corinthians 15:6 probably see Him at this eighth appearance. We base this assumption on several pieces of evidence. First, the angel told the women that Jesus would meet His followers in Galilee. Second, Matthew comments (28:17) that some doubt they actually saw the Lord Jesus alive, possibly thinking they had seen a ghost as the ten disciples thought when the Lord first stood among them (Luke 24:36–37). Third, Jesus had prearranged the meeting place. Getting this size of a crowd together would necessitate planning. On the other hand, if we've made the wrong assumption, we simply have eleven recorded appearances of Christ rather than ten, giving us even more evidence that Christ indeed rose from the dead.

APPEARANCE	MATTHEW	MARK	LUKE	JOHN	OTHER
1		16:9–11		20:11–18	
2	28:9–10				
3		16:12–13	24:13–32		
4			24:33–35		1 Cor. 15:5
5		16:14	24:36–43	20:19–25	
6				20:26–31	1 Cor. 15:5
7				21:1–25	
8	28:16–20	16:15–18			1 Cor. 15:6
9					1 Cor. 15:7
10			24:44–49		Acts 1:3–8

Scripture devotes only five words to the ninth appearance, "Then He appeared to James." We find these words in 1 Corinthians 15:7, not in the Gospels. The James spoken of here probably refers to the half-brother of Jesus, which would explain his presence in the upper room before Pentecost (Acts 1:14) and his becoming the leader of the church in Jerusalem (Acts 12:17; 15:13; 21:18), even though he previously did not believe in Jesus as the Messiah (John 7:5).

The tenth and last recorded appearance of Jesus before His ascension into heaven occurs in Jerusalem on the fortieth day of His resurrected ministry. He tells His followers to stay in Jerusalem until He clothes them with the power of the Holy Spirit (Luke 24:49; Acts 1:4–5).

After Jesus tells them to wait in Jerusalem until the Holy Spirit comes on them, Jesus leads them a Sabbath's walk to the Mount of Olives toward Bethany (Luke 24:50; Acts 1:12). There, as He blesses them, He begins to rise into the air. We call this event **the ascension**. Even after a cloud causes Jesus to disappear from sight, the disciples continue to stare. Who wouldn't? As they gaze intently into the sky, two angels appear, promising that just as Jesus ascended into heaven that day, so would He return to earth in the same way. Overwhelmed with joy, the disciples return to Jerusalem.

CONFIDENCE BUILDER #3

THE ASCENSION

| Mark 16:19–20 | Luke 24:50–53 | Acts 1:9–12 |

Now let's look more closely at where the above events occur.

WHERE?

With the exception of the seventh, eighth, and maybe the ninth appearances, every event recorded in Scripture during the Triumphant Period of Christ occurs in and around **Jerusalem**. The maps and chart below visually orient us to the approximate location of each confidence builder.

Let's start with the first two visits to the empty tomb. We do not know where the women spent Saturday night, but most scholars tend to place the women, with the exception of Joanna, staying somewhere in the southwest section of Jerusalem (1). Whether they stay in the same house or not, Scripture gives no clue. Scholars tend to have Joanna coming from Herod Antipas' Jerusalem palace (2). The entire group converges at the tomb with Mary arriving first (3). The women leave the tomb to report the empty tomb to the apostles (4). Peter and John run to the tomb to discover it empty (5) and then return to where they had spent the night (6).

Visits to the Empty Tomb and Jesus' Appearances

Mary Magdalene and the other women return to the tomb, where Jesus appears to them (7). Later that afternoon Jesus appears to Cleopas and another unnamed disciple on the road to Emmaus (8). At some point during the afternoon Jesus appears to Peter, but Scripture does not tell us where. That evening Jesus appears to the apostles minus Thomas (9). Eight days later Jesus appears to the apostles with Thomas present (10).

Several days later Jesus appears to seven of the disciples while they fish on the Sea of Galilee (11), which Scripture also calls the Sea of Tiberias (John 21:1). In the province of Galilee at a predetermined mountain, Jesus appears to the eleven disciples and possibly at this time to more than five hundred others mentioned in 1 Corinthians 15:6 (12). The action returns to Jerusalem where Jesus once again appears to His disciples (13) and then leads them out to the Mount of Olives where they watch as the living Lord ascends into heaven (14).

CONFIDENCE BUILDER	EVENT	COMMENTS	LOCATION
The Resurrection	Mary Magdalene and the women visit the empty tomb	They travel from where they spent the night to the tomb and back to the apostles	Jerusalem
	Peter and John visit the empty tomb	They travel from where they spent the night to the tomb and back to the apostles	Jerusalem
The Appearances	To Mary	During her second trip to the tomb	Jerusalem
	To the other women	During their second trip to the tomb	Jerusalem
	To Cleopas and another unnamed disciple	Traveling on the road from Jerusalem west to Emmaus	Emmaus

	To Peter	Scripture gives no details	Jerusalem
	To the apostles without Thomas	While the two from Emmaus describe seeing Jesus alive	Jerusalem
	To the apostles including Thomas	Eight days after the above appearance	Jerusalem
	To the seven apostles after they fished	Sea of Galilee, also known as the Sea of Tiberias	Sea of Galilee
	To the Eleven and maybe five hundred others	Scripture does not reveal the specific mountain	At a designated mountain in Galilee
	To James, the half-brother of Jesus	Scripture provides no clue	?
	To the disciples	As they walk from Jerusalem to the Mount of Olives	Jerusalem
The Ascension	Jesus rises into heaven	About a half mile from Jerusalem	Mount of Olives, east of Jerusalem

Now that we have a better understanding of where everything occurred during the Triumphant Period of Christ, let's look more closely at when each event happens.

WHEN?

The following chart gives a general overview of when each confidence builder occurs. Obviously, the resurrection takes place on the first day, Christ's ascension into heaven occurs on the last, and all the appearances occur between these two momentous events. Yet how do we know that the Triumphant Period of Christ lasts a total of only forty days? Nowhere in the Gospels do we read of how many days Christ walks on earth after His resurrection.

THE TRIUMPHANT PERIOD

CONFIDENCE BUILDER	DAY
Christ's resurrection	1
Christ's appearances	1–40
Christ's ascension	40

We find the answer not in the Gospels, but in Acts 1:3. Luke writes, "To these [the apostles] He also presented Himself alive, after His suffering, by many convincing proofs, appearing to them over a period of **forty days**." Let's look at the evidence given in Scripture of when Christ appears each time. The clues fall into four major categories.

The first category of clues relates to the events occurring on the first day. Each Gospel writer (Matthew 28:1; Mark 16:2; Luke 24:1; John 20:1) uses the phrase "the first day of the week" before launching into a description of the resurrection of Christ and His first five appearances. John shows the end of the first day in John 20:19 when he says, "When therefore it was evening, on that day, the first day of the week." After noting the time of day, he paints the scene of Christ appearing to the apostles minus Thomas.

The next category refers to Christ's appearance to the apostles with the addition of doubting Thomas. John gives the clue that allows us to pinpoint the day of this sixth appearance. He writes, "And after eight days again His disciples were inside, and Thomas with them."

Clues for the sixth and seventh appearances comprise the third category. We have several pieces of evidence to help determine on what days these appearances occur. Some clues come from Scripture; one, however, comes from an understanding of the geography of Palestine. We know from John 21:1 and Matthew 28:16 that the two appearances in question take place in Galilee rather than Jerusalem. Geographically, it takes about three days to traverse the small country of Palestine. If the disciples leave Jerusalem for Galilee the morning of the tenth day, they would have arrived *no earlier* than day twelve. If they went fishing on that very evening (John 21:3–4), the seventh appearance of Jesus occurs on the morning of day thirteen. Similarly, if they return to Jerusalem on day forty, they would have left Galilee *no later* than day thirty-eight.

CONFIDENCE BUILDER	EVENT	DAY	CLUE
The Resurrection	Mary Magdalene and women visit empty tomb	1	"On the first day of the week" (John 20:1)
	Peter and John visit the empty tomb	1	"On the first day of the week" (John 20:1)
The Appearances	1. To Mary	1	"On the first day of the week" (John 20:1)
	2. To the other women	1	"And very early on the first day of the week, they" (Mary Magdalene, Mary the mother of James, and Salome) (Mark 16:1–2)
	3. To Cleopas and another unnamed disciple	1	"And behold, two of them were going that very day" (Luke 24:13)
	4. To Peter	1	"It is getting toward evening . . . returned . . . found gathered together the eleven and those who were with them, saying, 'The Lord . . . appeared to Simon.'" (Luke 24:29–34)
	5. To the apostles without Thomas	1	"When therefore it was evening, on that day, the first day of the week" (John 20:19)

	6. To the apostles including Thomas	9	"And after eight days again His disciples were inside, and Thomas with them." (John 20:26)
	7. To the seven apostles after they fished	Between days 13 and 38	"After these things Jesus manifested Himself again to the disciples at the Sea of Tiberias . . . but when the day was now breaking" (John 21:1, 4)
	8. To the Eleven and maybe five hundred others	Between days 13 and 38	"But the eleven disciples proceeded to Galilee, to the mountain." (Matthew 28:16)
	9. To James, the half-brother of Jesus	?	(Scripture provides no evidence)
	10. To the disciples	40	"And He led them out as far as Bethany . . . and it came about that while He was blessing them, He parted from them." (Luke 24:50–51)
The Ascension	Jesus rises into heaven	40	"Appearing to them over a period of forty days" (Acts 1:3)

The last category of clues identifies the day when the last appearance and ascension happen. As we have already seen, Luke tells us that Jesus appeared to His followers over a period of forty days. So the last appearance, which involves Christ's ascension into heaven, occurs on day forty.

WHY?

We have clearly seen God's heart for the nations in the previous three periods of the Coming of Christ Era. Yet in the Triumphant Period of Christ the overall theme of the Bible—**God receiving glory by restoring fellowship between the nations and Himself through His Son, Jesus Christ**—becomes clear. As if shining a heavenly searchlight on the nations, all four Gospels quote Jesus telling His followers to take the message of God's love and forgiveness to all peoples. Jesus consistently mandates that His followers take the good news of eternal life to the ends of the earth—during the beginning, middle, and end of the Triumphant Period. So strongly does the risen Lord Jesus emphasize the nations during the forty days between His resurrection and ascension that these verses have become known as the Great Commission verses. Let's identify each of these passages.

Jesus first issues the Great Commission on the evening of the first day of His resurrection. In a room behind shut doors Jesus meets with the apostles (without Thomas), the two disciples from Emmaus, and, as Luke describes, "And those who were with them" (Luke 24:33). John 20:21 records Jesus' words, "Peace be with you; as the Father has sent Me, I also send you." Just as Christ labored to introduce people to a personal relationship with God, He has sends His followers to do the same.

The next two Great Commission mandates are given during the middle of Christ's Triumphant Period, somewhere between days thirteen and thirty-eight. At the mountain in Galilee (Matthew 28:16–17) with the five hundred mentioned in 1 Corinthians 15:6 probably in atten- dance, Jesus commands His followers in Matthew 28:19, "Go therefore and make disciples of all the nations, baptizing them in the name of the Father and the Son and the Holy Spirit." At this same rendezvous Jesus most likely makes the statement found in Mark 16:15, "Go into all the world and preach the gospel to all creation." Putting the two verses together, we could say that we as followers of Christ must go to every people group in the world and explain to each person in that group how they can have a personal relationship with God through faith in the Lord Jesus Christ.

GREAT COMMISSION VERSES

VERSE	DAY	FOCUS
John 20:21	1	Christ—our example
Matthew 28:19	Between 13 and 38	All people groups—our goal
Mark 16:15	Between 13 and 38	All individuals—our goal
Luke 24:46–47	40	The gospel—our message
Acts 1:8	40	The Holy Spirit—our enabling power

The Lord Jesus gives the Great Commission again on day forty, at the end of His earthly ministry. In Luke 24:46–47 Luke quotes Jesus, "Thus it is written, that the Christ should suffer and rise again from the dead the third day; and that repentance for forgiveness of sins should be proclaimed in His name to all the nations, beginning from Jerusalem." In two simple verses Jesus summarizes the message of the entire Bible. As humans, we have a serious problem. Our *sins* have cut us off from a relationship with God. But in His mercy and grace, God provided a remedy for our fatal flaw: *the Christ should suffer and rise again from the dead the third day.* Yet for us to take advantage of this remedy for our sins, we must agree with God that our sins are evil, and we must believe that Christ died as payment for our sins. We must turn from our sins (repentance) and turn to Christ for salvation (faith).

Christ last announces the Great Commission just before He ascends into heaven on day forty. Luke records His words in Acts 1:8, "But you shall receive power when the Holy Spirit has come upon you; and you shall be My witnesses both in Jerusalem, and in all Judea and Samaria, and even to the remotest part of the earth." This last Great Commission verse shows us the power needed to accomplish such a huge task—the

Holy Spirit. In the next chapter we will see how the believers appropriate this power.

Let's turn now to the last of the four Gospel writers.

WHO?

Having looked at Matthew, Mark, and Luke in the previous chapters, we now come to **John**. What does the Scripture teach us about him?

Interestingly, we know a lot about John's family. Born to Zebedee and possibly Salome, he becomes a fisherman, working on the Sea of Galilee with James (Mark 1:19), his brother who is later martyred by sword at the command of Herod Agrippa (Acts 12:2). If we compare Matthew 27:56, Mark 15:40, and John 19:25, it appears Salome may have been the mother of James and John, as well as the sister of Jesus' mother, making James and John cousins of Jesus. The family seems to have achieved a fairly high level of success because their business uses hired servants (Mark 1:20) and has connections with the high priest in Jerusalem (John 18:15).

Realize that during those days religious people had their favorite Bible teachers just as many people do today. In that culture, however, the teachers, called rabbis, taught only from the Old Testament, because God had not yet given the New Testament. John 1:35 tells us that at some point John had become a disciple of John the Baptist. During one of John's visits to listen to his favorite rabbi, John hears John the Baptist identify Jesus as the Lamb of God. From that day on, John follows Jesus.

We see John's devotion to the Messiah when Scripture mentions him as the first of the twelve apostles to follow Jesus and the last to leave Him after the Messiah's arrest in the garden of Gethsemane. Instead of fleeing with the other disciples, John along with Peter follow Christ all the way to the court of the high priest (John 18:15). Only John of all the

Twelve witnesses the crucifixion, an action extremely dangerous for any male follower of this man accused of wanting to overthrow Caesar (John 19:26, 27). John also arrives first at the empty tomb after hearing Mary Magdalene's report (John 20:4). And while he fished with some other disciples, John is the first to recognize the resurrected Jesus standing on the beach (John 21:7).

In the years following Christ's ascension into heaven, John becomes a leader of the fledgling church in Jerusalem (Galatians 2:9). Later he moves to Ephesus (located in modern-day Turkey) where he serves as bishop. He suffers persecution when the Romans under Domitian exile him to the island of Patmos. Upon his release, tradition says that John returns to Ephesus where he dies around the end of the first century.

John's walk with his Lord radically changes his life and character. John begins as a hotheaded, arrogant young man wanting to call down fire on the Samaritans (Mark 3:17; Luke 9:54–56) and asking to sit next to Christ in glory (Mark 10:35–38). Yet as he follows Christ, he becomes known as the apostle of love.

Whereas Matthew and Mark write one Gospel each, and Luke writes one Gospel and the book of Acts, John pens five books of the New Testament: the Gospel of John, three epistles, and Revelation.

WRITINGS OF JOHN

Gospel of John
1 John
2 John
3 John
Revelation

John's Gospel contains several unique characteristics. All but four chapters take place during a Jewish feast, providing important clues to when events occur during the ministry of Christ. The four chapters that do not occur during feasts focus on individuals: John the Baptist in chapter one, the woman at the well in chapter four, Lazarus in chapter eleven, and Peter in chapter twenty-one. The Gospel of John also uniquely focuses on the words of the Lord Jesus Christ by highlighting nine times that Jesus elaborated on the phrase "I am," a clear reference to being God (Exodus 3:13–14).

NINE STATEMENTS (WORDS) IN JOHN'S GOSPEL

I am He	John 4:26; 8:24; 13:19
I am the bread of life	John 6:35
I am the light of the world	John 8:12; 9:5
I am the door of the sheep	John 10:7, 9
I am the good shepherd	John 10:11, 14
I am the Son of God	John 10:36
I am the resurrection and the life	John 11:25
I am the way, the truth, and the life	John 14:6
I am the true vine	John 15:1

Anyone, however, can claim divinity, and words are cheap unless backed by actions. Jesus even concedes this point. That's why He says to one of His disciples in John 14:10–11, "Do you not believe that I am in the Father, and the Father is in Me? The words that I say to you I do not speak on My own initiative, but the Father abiding in Me does His works. Believe Me that I am in the Father, and the Father in Me; otherwise believe on account of the works themselves." But what works? In his Gospel, John highlights seven miracles in addition to the resurrection itself.

SEVEN SIGNS (WORKS) IN JOHN'S GOSPEL

Turns water into wine	John 2:1–10
Heals a royal official's son	John 4:46–54
Heals a lame man	John 5:1–9
Feeds 5,000	John 6:1–14
Walks on water	John 6:16–21
Heals a man blind from birth	John 9:1–11
Raises Lazarus from the dead	John 11:1–44

John clearly echoes the words of Jesus (John 10:37, 38) when he declares in John 20:30–31 that he wrote about these miracles so that we might believe Jesus is the Christ, the Son of God, and that by believing we might have life in His name.

Take a look at the following chart where we identify the reasons John wrote two of his five New Testament books. In his Gospel, John clearly communicates his desire for people to have eternal life by believing in Jesus Christ, the Son of God. Yet he doesn't stop there. In his first epistle he goes a step further. He not only wants people to have eternal life but he also wants them to confidently know that they have it. In other words, he wants them to have an assurance that they now possess a right relationship with God through their faith in Christ.

BOOK'S TITLE	BOOK'S PURPOSE
The Gospel According to John	"But these [signs] have been written that you may believe that Jesus is the Christ, the Son of God; and that believing you may have life in His name." (John 20:31)
The First Epistle of John	"These things I have written to you who believe in the name of the Son of God, in order that you may know that you have eternal life." (1 John 5:13)

The apostle John explains how a person inherits eternal life in the well-known verse John 3:16. In this verse, the Lord Jesus says to Nicodemus, "For God so loved the world, that He gave His only begotten Son, that whoever believes in Him should not perish, but have eternal life." This verse summarizes the good news of God's love and forgiveness in four statements. To help you remember them, think *up, down, up, down*.

THE GOSPEL SUMMARIZED

Up	God's Purpose	For God so loved the world
Down	Man's Problem	Should not perish, but have eternal life
Up	God's Remedy	That He gave His only begotten Son
Down	Man's Response	That whoever believes in Him

Many cultural Christians insist that they believe in Jesus. Yet the word *believe* in our English language has two meanings: believing from the head and believing from the heart. The Greek word for *believe* in John 3:16 refers to the latter connotation. Believing from the heart and not just the head moves a person from being a cultural Christian to being a biblical Christian.

FOR NEXT TIME

If you are having an extremely busy week:	If you have a little extra time:	If you can't get enough:
read Acts 1–2.	add 1 Peter.	add 2 Peter.

PERIOD #5

PERIOD #5

The Church's Private Period

We've now completed our examination of the first of two New Testament historical eras, the Coming of Christ Era, which the Old Testament Scriptures long anticipated. The Coming of Christ Era focuses on the private, public, trials, and triumphant periods of Christ's life. By harmonizing accounts of the four Gospels—Matthew, Mark, Luke, and John—we gained a chronological understanding of Jesus' birth, life, ministry, crucifixion, resurrection, and ascension. Hopefully, much of the border of the New Testament puzzle has begun taking shape.

In this chapter we begin assembling the part of the New Testament puzzle that concentrates on the Church. We move from reading the Gospels to reading the book of Acts. Interestingly, the time periods that compose the history of the Church in the book of Acts convey the same emphases as the time periods comprising the historical era of Christ. So, we have assigned them the same four names.

In order to maintain the big picture, recall the names of the two New Testament eras, the four periods pertaining to the Lord Jesus, and the four periods that organize the Church's history. Remember that the names of the last four periods mirror the names of the first four periods.

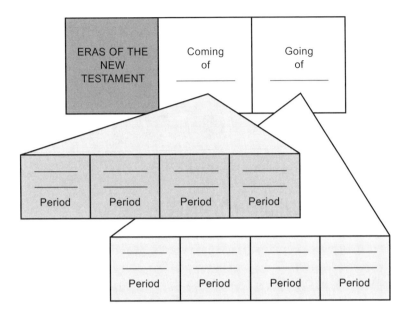

The four time periods spanning the Coming of Christ Era contain twenty-four key items: seven groups of people summarize the early years of Jesus; seven themes capture His public ministry; seven days encompass the Passion Week (the last week before the crucifixion) of Jesus; and three confidence builders result from the Lord's final forty days on earth. Try not to look back at past chapters as you identify these key items in the following chart. Remember that mastering all twenty-four items will help you acquire a firm grip on the first part of the New Testament.

CHRIST'S PRIVATE PERIOD: 7 GROUPS	CHRIST'S PUBLIC PERIOD: 7 THEMES	CHRIST'S TRIALS PERIOD: 7 DAYS
Born to _____ and _____	Inspires the _____	_____ occurs on Sunday
Worshiped by _____	Instructs the _____	_____ occurs on Monday
Honored by _____ and _____	Infuriates the _____	_____ occurs on Tuesday
Sought by _____ and _____	Causes _____	_____ occurs on Wednesday
Taught by temple _____	Cures the _____	_____ and _____ occur on Thursday
Baptized by _____	Casts out _____	_____ occurs on Friday
Tempted by _____	Reveals that we can be _____	_____ occurs on Saturday

CHRIST'S TRIUMPHANT PERIOD: 3 CONFIDENCE BUILDERS
_____
_____
_____

The ascension of the Lord Jesus into heaven ends one biblical era and launches another. The Coming of Christ Era comes to a close, and the Going of the Church begins.

WHAT?

Throughout His ministry, Jesus explains to His followers God's heart for the nations. For the forty days of the Triumphant Period, however, He repeatedly stresses—in what we call the Great Commission verses—the Church's responsibility to *go* as His witnesses to all the nations, proclaiming the good news of eternal life. In Matthew 28:19, the Son of God commands His followers, "*Go* therefore and make disciples of all the nations." In Mark 16:15, the Lord mandates the Church, "*Go* into all the world and preach the gospel to all creation" (emphasis added). With Jesus ascending into heaven, the time has come. A new era has begun—the Going of the Church.

Yet the Church doesn't begin her task immediately. In obedience to Christ's final instructions, His followers wait until they receive the necessary power to fulfill their responsibility. This time of waiting serves as a time of **preparation of the Church**, much like Christ's thirty years of preparation before His public ministry.

THE CHURCH'S PRIVATE PERIOD

Acts 1:12–2:4

Luke, the author of the book of Acts, devotes only parts of two chapters to the Private Period of the Church: Acts 1:12–2:4. He packs, however, these nineteen verses full of information. Follow along as God prepares His people to take the message of His love and forgiveness to the nations.

HOW?

After watching the Lord Jesus ascend into heaven, the followers of Christ leave the Mount of Olives and return to Jerusalem (Acts 1:12). You can just imagine their conversation as they make the short walk back to the city, a conversation undoubtedly repeated many times in the ensuing years as they reminisced about witnessing the Lord float into the clouds.

For the next week and a half they wait in obedience to their Lord's command: "And behold, I am sending forth the promise of My Father upon you; but you are to stay in the city until you are clothed with power from on high" (Luke 24:49). What happens during this time of waiting? Three events: the disciples return to pray, they replace Judas, and they receive the Holy Spirit.

THREE EVENTS

Return to pray	Acts 1:12–14
Replace Judas	Acts 1:15–26
Receive the Holy Spirit	Acts 2:1–4

With Jesus gone, the disciples' first order of business is to pray—a lot. Heading back toward Jerusalem, the followers of Christ **return to pray** in a private home. Others join them, soon crowding the upper room of the chosen house. Acts 1:14 describes the congregation as continually devoting themselves to prayer.

Several groups of people attend this extended prayer meeting. The twelve apostles, minus Judas, take center stage (Acts 1:13). Women also arrive, most likely those who had visited the empty tomb; this group may have also included the wives of the apostles as well as other women. The earthly family of the Lord prominently ranks among those in attendance. Luke mentions Mary the mother of Jesus and Jesus' half-brothers (Acts 1:14), who initially did not believe in Jesus as the promised Messiah but changed their minds and hearts after the resurrection. Joseph, the stepfather of Jesus, remains notably absent from the family members, perhaps because he had already died. Interestingly, this passage marks the last time Scripture speaks of Jesus' mother. Additional followers raise the total number in the upper room to 120 believers (Acts 1:15).

On one of these days of waiting—Scripture does not specify which day—Peter quotes from Psalms 69 and 109 (Acts 1:16, 20) to show that this group must **replace Judas** to fill the place among the Twelve that he abdicated (see Matthew 19:28). Recall that Judas on Wednesday of the Passion Week betrays the Lord Jesus for thirty pieces of silver. Two days later he feels overwhelming remorse and hangs himself. Our current passage in Acts adds a couple more details to the events surrounding Judas's death. Apparently, after Judas hanged himself, the rope or branch broke. Upon hitting the ground, the force of the impact ruptures Judas's body, causing his bowels to gush out (Acts 1:18). Peter hints at Judas's ultimate destination (Acts 1:25) when he declares that Judas had turned aside to go to his own place.

Having identified the need to replace Judas, Peter communicates the criterion the successor must meet: The replacement must have accompanied the other apostles from the time of John the Baptist until the time of Christ's ascension (Acts 1:22). In other words, the new apostle needed to have witnessed the entire public ministry of Jesus and His post-resurrection appearances (Acts 1:21). This prerequisite would furnish the necessary credibility for the new apostle to proclaim the resurrection of the Christ with authority.

After establishing personal experience of Christ's entire ministry as the requirement for apostleship, the assembly nominates two people, Barsabbas (meaning "son of the Sabbath," probably because his birth occurred on a Sabbath) and Matthias (Acts 1:23). To break the tie, the people pray and then draw lots (Proverbs 16:33), thus selecting Matthias. This event marks the last time followers of Christ use this Old Testament practice of drawing lots to determine God's will (Acts 1:26).

Though the followers of Christ spend ten days in the upper room praying and choosing Judas's replacement, more than anything else they spend the time waiting in obedience to the Lord Jesus Christ's command to stay in the city until He empowers them. Even though the disciples could not anticipate the quality and quantity of the power that God would manifest in and through their lives on the day of Pentecost, they certainly understood *how* He would empower them.

Jesus made two statements that revealed the source. In Luke 24:49, the Lord explained that His Father would clothe them with power. He further added in Acts 1:8 that they would receive power when the Holy Spirit came upon them. These comments of Christ reminded the disciples of the Old Testament passage in Joel 2:28–32. We know this because, on the day of Pentecost, Peter quotes it: "'And it shall be in the last days,' God says, 'That I will pour forth of My Spirit upon all mankind; . . . I will in those days pour forth of My Spirit and they shall prophesy. . . . And it shall be, that everyone who calls on the name of the Lord shall be saved'" (Acts 2:17–21). Jesus had made it abundantly clear that He would soon empower them with the Holy Spirit whom God had promised six centuries earlier. God fulfills that promise on the day of Pentecost.

Suddenly, the loud noise of a violent rushing wind—imagine a tornado—fills the entire house, announcing the arrival of the Father's promise (Acts 2:2). To everyone's amazement, what appears to be tongues of fire rest on each one as the Holy Spirit fills the followers of Christ. After the disciples **receive the Holy Spirit**, they begin to speak in languages other than their own (Acts 2:4), which adds to the wonder of this incredible experience. The purpose of these languages becomes evident after they exit the Church's Private Period and enter the Church's Public Period. But that's for the next chapter.

Let's now consider where and when the events of the Church's Private Period take place.

WHERE?

All the events occurring during this period of the Going of the Church Era take place in a localized area in and around **Jerusalem**. The Church's Private Period begins with the followers of Christ standing on the Mount of Olives (1), gazing intently into the sky where the Lord Jesus had just ascended and disappeared into a cloud. Two angels appear and tell them that Jesus will return to earth in this same way. After this they return to Jerusalem (Acts 1:12). We know how far they travel back to the city because Luke notes the distance as a Sabbath's day journey. Over the years rabbis had developed a tradition, based on Exodus 16:29 and Numbers 35:5, that a person could walk on a Sabbath no farther than two thousand cubits. A cubit equals eighteen inches, so two thousand cubits measures three thousand feet, or a little over half of a mile.

Upon returning to the city, they enter an upper room (2). We don't know the exact location of this upper room or who owned it. Regardless, for the next week and a half, the activity of the fledgling Church centers in this room with the exception of periodic trips to the temple (Luke 24:52–53).

The Church's Private Period

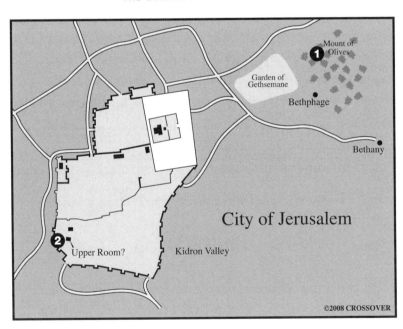

PUTTING TOGETHER THE PUZZLE OF THE NEW TESTAMENT

Now let's seek to determine when the Church's Private Period occurs.

WHEN?

The Private Period of the Church covers the least amount of time in the Going of the Church Era. It lasted for only **ten days**. How do we arrive at this duration? It takes a penchant for mathematics.

Let's first determine when the Private Period ends. Scripture provides the answer in Acts 2:1. The Private Period ends on the day of Pentecost, the day when the Holy Spirit fills the followers of Christ.

Now what do we know about Pentecost? Almost fifteen hundred years earlier, Moses had directed the Jewish people to celebrate seven holy convocations (Leviticus 23:4–44) in this order: Passover, Unleavened Bread, First Fruits, Pentecost, Trumpets, Atonement, and Tabernacles. The Feast of Pentecost occurred seven weeks after the Feast of First Fruits (Leviticus 23:15), or fifty days after the first Sabbath that followed the Feast of Passover (Leviticus 23:16).

When we refer to the chart below and identify the days on which the crucifixion, resurrection, and ascension of Christ occur, the time frame of the Church's Private Period begins to come clearly into focus. We know the soldiers crucified the Lord Jesus on Passover, which fell that year on a Friday, the day before the Jewish Sabbath. We also know that God the Father raised the Lord Jesus Christ from the dead on the following Sunday, which interestingly fell on the day marked for the Feast of First Fruits (Leviticus 23:9–11; 1 Corinthians 15:20). Finally, we know from the clue found in Acts 1:3 that Christ walked on earth for forty days until He ascended into heaven.

SUNDAY	MONDAY	TUESDAY	WEDNESDAY	THURSDAY	FRIDAY	SATURDAY
					Crucifixion and *Passover*	*Jewish Sabbath*
Resurrection and *First Fruits*	2	3	4	5	6	7
8	9	10	11	12	13	14
15	16	17	18	19	20	21
22	23	24	25	26	27	28
29	30	31	32	33	34	35
36	37	38	39	40 Ascension	41	42
43	44	45	46	47	48	49
50 Pentecost						

With these markers now in place, we can determine the number of days that the followers of Christ spent waiting in the upper room. Subtracting the forty days of Christ's post-resurrection ministry from the fifty total days gives us a total of ten complete days.

WHY?

As we saw earlier in the How? section, the early Christians might not understand what God's enabling power might look like, but they do know how He will empower them. Additionally, they know why Christ will empower them: so they can serve as effective *witnesses* of His *resurrection* to all the *nations*.

Recall the words Jesus speaks in Luke 24:46–48 before He instructs His followers to wait in the city until He empowers them. He proclaims, "Thus it is written, that the Christ should suffer and *rise again* from the dead the third day; and that repentance for forgiveness of sins should be proclaimed in His name to all the *nations*, beginning from Jerusalem. You are *witnesses* of these things" (emphasis added). Peter reminds the people in the upper room of this responsibility as they prepare to replace Judas, saying in Acts 1:22, "One of these should become a *witness* with us *of His resurrection*" (emphasis added). They must make Christ's last command their first concern.

For people to experience God's love and forgiveness—or as Peter puts it, to "be saved" (Acts 2:21)—the tiny band of believers knows that they need to serve as effective witnesses of Christ's resurrection. They realize that they need to proclaim the good news of Christ in order for the nations to hear and respond in faith. Christ had made it perfectly clear that He had chosen them to participate in the overall theme of the Bible: **God receiving glory by restoring fellowship between the nations and Himself through His Son, Jesus Christ.** To accomplish such a God-sized task, they require God-sized power, a resource God makes available to them at Pentecost.

Turn your attention now to the fifth of the eight New Testament authors, the fisherman turned preacher, who on the day of Pentecost powerfully witnesses of the resurrection of Jesus.

WHO?

In the previous four chapters we learned about the writers of the Gospels: Matthew, Mark, Luke, and John. Now we turn to Peter who, along with Paul, serves as a pillar of the early Church. We will look first at his life and then at his writings.

The Bible goes into quite a bit of detail about Peter. Over two hundred verses refer to him by one of his three names: Simon, his Jewish given name; Cephas, the Aramaic name given to him by the Lord Jesus; and Peter, the Greek translation of Cephas, meaning "rock."

From these verses we know a lot about his immediate family. We know his father carries the name of Jona or John, because Jesus refers to Peter as Simon Barjona (Matthew 16:17). *Bar* means "son of," much like the surname Johnson, or "son of John." Peter makes his living as a fisherman with Andrew, his younger brother, possibly in partnership with James and John, the sons of Zebedee. Originally from Bethsaida, he lives in Capernaum with his wife (Matthew 8:14). After Pentecost he apparently moves to Jerusalem (Galatians 2:1, 9) until he begins his missionary journeys. While on these missionary trips, his wife travels with him (1 Corinthians 9:5).

Scripture also provides a tremendous amount of information about Peter's relationship with the Lord. Andrew first introduces him to Christ near where John the Baptist was ministering (John 1:40–42). Approximately a year later, while fishing on the shores of the Sea of Galilee, Peter has another encounter with Jesus. Jesus commands Peter to follow Him and become a fisher of men. Peter, along with Andrew, James, and John, leaves everything and begins an incredible life-long adventure of following the Son of God (Luke 5:1–11). A few months later Jesus calls Peter to serve as one of the twelve disciples (Luke 6:13–14), and he soon becomes the leading spokesman for them.

Apart from Judas's betrayal of Jesus, few actions of the disciples have become as famous as those of Peter. Christians around the world learn about trusting the Lord by reading of Peter walking on the water (Matthew 14:28–31). Peter utters the confession, "Thou art the Christ, the Son of the living God" (Matthew 16:16–18), on which Christ builds His Church. He insists that even if he has to die with Christ, he will not deny Him (Mark 14:31), though he does deny his Lord at least three times. Peter races to the empty tomb the moment he hears Mary

Magdalene's report (John 20:4). He dives off the boat and swims to shore when the seven disciples recognize the risen Lord Jesus standing on the beach (John 21:7).

After walking with his Master and being filled with the Holy Spirit, Peter soon epitomizes the name that Christ had given him—his commitment to Christ becomes *rock solid*. He serves as the first leader of the Church in Jerusalem. His passionate sermons spread the message of God's love and forgiveness to thousands (Acts 2:41; 4:4). The Jewish religious authorities repeatedly imprison him (Acts 4:3; 5:18; 12:4) and beat him (Acts 5:40), yet his faith remains unshakable. Ultimately, his love for the Lord Jesus leads him to a cross (John 21:18–19). Tradition says that he asked the Roman soldiers to crucify him upside down because he felt unworthy to die as Christ had died.

Peter serves not only as a preacher but also as a writer, penning the two epistles that bear his name: 1 Peter and 2 Peter. These two small books consist of only eight total chapters. The first book gives special attention to troubles coming from outside the Church in the form of persecution of the growing Christian movement. The second book deals more with troubles taking place inside the Church caused by the heresy of false teachers.

WRITINGS OF PETER

1 Peter	Focuses on troubles outside the Church	Endure hardships
2 Peter	Focuses on troubles inside the Church	Eliminate heresy

We can summarize the first epistle of Peter in four words: salvation, submission, suffering, and service. Peter exhorts his readers to grow in salvation by longing for the pure milk of the Word of God (1 Peter 2:2). In the second part of his book he deals with submission in the realms of government, business, and marriage. He takes suffering in this life for granted but explains that we must suffer for doing right rather than for doing wrong (1 Peter 3:17). Finally, Peter implores the elders of the Church to serve by properly shepherding the people of God (1 Peter 5:2). Throughout the book Peter uses the term *precious*, a term that refers to the incredible value of something. He describes as precious our faith (1 Peter 1:7), Christ's blood (1 Peter 1:19), Christ as the living cornerstone (1 Peter 2:4–7), and a gentle spirit (1 Peter 3:4).

OUTLINE OF 1 PETER

Salvation	1:1–2:12
Submission	2:13–3:12
Suffering	3:13–4:19
Service	5:1–14

In his second epistle, Peter first traces the path to Christian usefulness and fruitfulness. He then goes on to warn against the destructiveness of heresy. Finally, he explains the delay in Christ's return.

OUTLINE OF 2 PETER

Description of spiritual growth	Chapter 1
Danger of false teachers	Chapter 2
Day of Christ's return	Chapter 3

FOR NEXT TIME

If you are having an extremely busy week:	If you have a little extra time:	If you can't get enough:
read Acts 2–21.	add Romans and Galatians.	add 1 and 2 Corinthians and 1 and 2 Thessalonians.

PERIOD #6

PERIOD #6

The Church's Public Period

The departure of Christ started a new historical era: the Going of the Church. As we trace the development of the Church in the New Testament, we discover it follows a pattern similar to the life of Christ. We saw in the previous chapter that the Church began just as the earthly life of the Son of God began, basically out of the public's eye.

Once again let's review this historical symmetry.

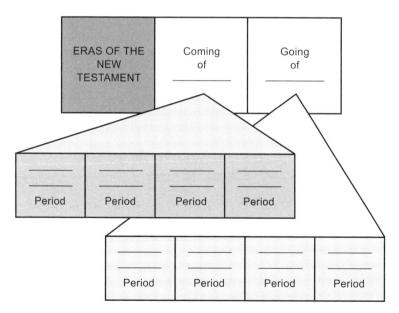

Moving from general to the specifics, recall that the four time periods covering the life of Christ contain twenty-four key items: seven groups; seven themes; seven days; and three confidence builders. The first period of the Church also contains only three key items giving us a bit of a break to shore up any weak areas in mastering the other key items. Take the time to fill in the following chart that organizes all of our key items.

CHRIST'S _____ PERIOD: 7 GROUPS	CHRIST'S _____ PERIOD: 7 THEMES	CHRIST'S _____ PERIOD: 7 DAYS
Born to _____ and _____	Inspires the _____	_____ occurs on Sunday
Worshiped by _____	Instructs the _____	_____ occurs on Monday
Honored by _____ and _____	Infuriates the _____	_____ occurs on Tuesday
Sought by _____ and _____	Causes _____	_____ occurs on Wednesday
Taught by temple _____	Cures the _____	_____ and _____ occur on Thursday
Baptized by _____	Casts out _____	_____ occurs on Friday
Tempted by _____	Reveals that we can be _____	_____ occurs on Saturday

CHRIST'S _____ PERIOD: 3 CONFIDENCE BUILDERS	CHURCH'S _____ PERIOD: 3 EVENTS
_____	_____
_____	_____
_____	_____

When we last left the followers of Christ, the Holy Spirit had just arrived and filled them with power so that they might take the message of God's love and forgiveness to the nations. Let's see what happens during the Church's Public Period.

WHAT?

In this period of New Testament history, the Church's Public Period, the followers of Christ begin to powerfully proclaim the blessing of God's love and forgiveness. The message of Christ's life, death, burial, and resurrection becomes the bold **proclamation of the Church** and covers twenty chapters of Scripture from Acts 2:5 to 21:26.

THE CHURCH'S PUBLIC PERIOD

Acts 2:5–21:26

Let's see how they bless the entire known world with the good news that Christ had risen from the dead.

HOW?

The newly empowered apostles take the biblical message of salvation to the nations in a series of **three advances**. Each advance has a different leader who focuses on a new cultural group. The initial advance, led by Peter, takes the gospel to the Jewish people in Jerusalem. The next advance, spearheaded by Philip the deacon (not Philip the apostle), successfully proclaims the resurrection of Christ to Samaritans. Because the Samaritans originated during the Old Testament times from Jews intermarrying with Gentiles, they represent a culture influenced by both Jewish and Gentile beliefs. Finally, the great apostle Paul carries the plan of salvation to Gentiles.

Let's consider more closely each advance, beginning with Peter's ministry to the Jews in Jerusalem. We read in the previous chapter that the noise of a violent rushing wind accompanies the arrival of the Holy Spirit as He fills the followers of Christ in the upper room. Apparently, in addition to the disciples, others hear the loud noise. A multitude that consists of local residents as well as Jews and proselytes (Gentiles who joined the Jewish faith) from fifteen other nations gathers near the wind's sound (Acts 2:6). As the people congregate, they hear the disciples speaking about the mighty deeds of God in their languages of origin, which understandably bewilders and amazes them (Acts 2:5, 6, 11). With the crowd growing to several thousand people (Acts 2:41), the assembly apparently moves to a part of the city with a large open area, possibly the temple.

Around the third hour of the day, or 9 A.M., **Peter** stands and preaches about the resurrection of the Lord Jesus Christ, launching **the first advance** of the gospel. To help the **Jews** better understand, he refers them to the prophecies about the coming Messiah contained in their Scriptures (Acts 2:25–28, 30–31, 34–35), which we know as the Old Testament. Peter's message pierces their hearts, so the Jewish listeners question Peter and the other apostles about the next step to take (Acts 2:37). Peter explains that they must repent in order to experience God's forgiveness for their disobedience (Acts 2:38). In other words, they must turn away from their sinful practices and turn to God by trusting in His Son the Messiah to make them right with God. Three thousand people respond (Acts 2:41).

Following Pentecost, the new Christ-followers devotedly spend their time listening to the apostles teach, fellowshipping with one another, eating together, and praying (Acts 2:42–45). They meet both in the temple and in private homes (Acts 2:46). During these days many more Jews come to faith in Jesus Christ (Acts 2:47).

On one of these days, around 3 P.M. Peter and John walk to the temple to pray. Along the way they meet a man lame from birth who daily begs for money at the Beautiful Gate (Acts 3:1–2). The beggar anticipates money when the two apostles focus their attention on him, but instead he receives healing in both his feet and ankles (Acts 3:3–7). Entering the temple, the beggar begins to leap as he praises God for the miracle brought to him in the name of Jesus (Acts 3:8).

Many of the worshipers recognize the exuberant, forty-plus-year-old man (Acts 4:22) as the one who regularly sits at the gate begging for money. As an amazed crowd gathers around the healed man and the two apostles near the portico of Solomon, Peter uses the opportunity to preach a second message (Acts 3:9–12), highlighting the fact that God had raised Jesus from the dead (Acts 3:15). Using the Old Testament Scriptures as he did on Pentecost, Peter again shows that Jesus fulfilled the ancient prophecies of the promised Messiah (Acts 3:18, 21–24). Of those listening to Peter, five thousand men (Acts 4:4), not counting women and children, choose to believe his message; as a result, their sins are forgiven (Acts 3:19).

PETER'S FOUR SERMONS

PASSAGE	MESSAGE	O. T. PROPHECY	RESULT
Acts 2:14–41 (In the temple?)	"This Jesus *God raised* up again, to which *we are all witnesses*." (Acts 2:32)	"And so, because he was a prophet . . . he looked ahead and spoke of the resurrection of the Christ." (Ps. 16:10; Acts 2:30–31)	3,000 believe in Christ (Acts 2:41)
Acts 3:12–4:4 (In the temple)	"The Prince of Life, the one whom *God raised* from the dead, a fact to which *we are witnesses*." (Acts 3:15)	"But the things which God announced beforehand by the mouth of all the prophets, that His Christ should suffer, He has thus fulfilled." (Deut. 18:15; Acts 3:18)	5,000 believe in Christ; Peter and John in jail (Acts 4:4)
Acts 4:8–12 (Before the Sanhedrin)	"Jesus Christ the Nazarene, whom you crucified, whom *God raised* from the dead." (Acts 4:10)	"He [Jesus] is the stone which was rejected by you, the builders, but which became the very corner stone." (Ps. 118:22; Acts 4:11)	Threatened by the Sanhedrin, yet see (Acts 5:14)
Acts 5:29–32 (Before the Sanhedrin)	"The *God* of our fathers *raised* up Jesus, whom you had put to death by hanging Him on a cross. . . . And *we are witnesses* of these things." (Acts 5:30, 32)	(Not recorded)	Flogged by the Sanhedrin, yet see (Acts 6:7)

The message also produces a negative response, because it disturbs the temple priests, the captain of the guard whose authority came second only to the high priest, and the Sadducees. Remember that the Sadducees did not believe in the resurrection of the body or the immortality of the spirit. The religious leaders move into the crowd and arrest Peter and John. Because of the lateness of the hour and the illegality of night trials, the authorities throw the two apostles into jail (Acts 4:1–3).

The next day, the Sanhedrin—consisting of Caiaphas as the high priest (Acts 4:6) and his Council (Acts 4:15)—assembles in order to judge Peter and John (Acts 4:7, 9). Peter, filled with the Spirit (Acts 4:8), defends himself by preaching his third message. As before, he focuses on God raising Jesus Christ of Nazareth from the dead (Acts 4:10). Once again he uses the Old Testament to support the validity of his claim (Acts 4:11). This time, however, no one responds by believing in Christ as the Son of God. After the Sanhedrin commands the two apostles never again to speak or teach about the name of Jesus, the Jewish rulers release them (Acts 4:18–21).

Peter and John not only refuse to accept the Council's directive to cease speaking about Jesus but they also return to their companions and pray that God would give them even more confidence to proclaim the name of Christ (Acts 4:29). As the group prays, the Holy Spirit answers their prayers and fills them with the courage they need to continue to speak the word of God with boldness (Acts 4:31). With great power the apostles give witness to the resurrection of the Lord Jesus (Acts 4:33), adding to their number multitudes of believers (Acts 5:14).

In retaliation against the success of the growing movement, the jealous high priest and his associates put all the apostles in jail (Acts 5:17–18). That night an angel miraculously frees them and tells them to continue proclaiming the message of Life (Acts 5:19–20). The next day the Sanhedrin discovers that the apostles have inexplicably escaped from the jail and have returned to preaching in the temple

(Acts 5:22–25). Seizing them without force, the Council questions the apostles regarding their teaching about Jesus after they had been commanded to stop (Acts 5:26–28).

Peter answers the Council with his fourth recorded message. The apostle boldly communicates the good news of God's love and forgiveness by insisting that he and the others witnessed the risen Jesus, whom they (religious leaders) had put to death by hanging Him on a cross (Acts 5:29–32).

As with Peter's third message, his fourth message meets a negative response. After the Council discusses what sentence they should render on this renegade group of Galileans (Acts 5:33–39), they decide against slaying them and instead flog them. After the flogging, the Council releases the apostles with orders to speak no more in the name of Jesus (Acts 5:40). As before, the apostles decide to obey God rather than the Council and return to teaching and preaching Jesus as the Christ on a daily basis both in the temple and from house to house (Acts 5:42).

The first advance of the gospel led by Peter through his four messages proves quite successful—so successful in fact that the number of disciples greatly increases among the Jews in Jerusalem. The impact of this advance also leads many of the Jewish priests to believe in Jesus as the Messiah (Acts 6:7).

After the Jewish rulers stone a deacon named Stephen (Acts 6:8–7:60), a great persecution arises against the Church in Jerusalem, scattering all the followers of Christ—except for the apostles—throughout the regions surrounding the holy city (Acts 8:1). God uses the persecution to launch **the second advance** of the message of Christ, this one among Samaritans.

Philip, one of the deacons selected by the apostles to serve food to widows (Acts 6:1–5), leaves Jerusalem during the persecution and goes north to Samaria (Acts 8:5), where he begins boldly proclaiming Christ as well as healing the sick and casting out evil spirits. The **Samaritans** respond positively to his preaching and believe the good news.

When the apostles in Jerusalem hear that the despised Samaritans have received the word of God, they send Peter and John as their representatives to confirm whether the Samaritans have truly become believers in Christ (Acts 8:14). That the apostolic leaders have to validate the conversion of the Samaritans seems unnecessary, because Jesus had already demonstrated His love for them. (See page 64.) We must recall, however, the tense situation that had existed between Jews and Samaritans for over seven hundred years. Even though Jewish believers have *spiritually* experienced God's forgiveness for their sinful attitudes, they still *culturally* carry a tremendous amount of ungodly prejudice against Samaritans. The Lord must destroy this cultural barrier in order to bring unity to His Church. But how?

As Peter and John pray, the Samaritans receive the Holy Spirit in much the same way as the Jews received Him on the day of Pentecost (Acts 8:15–17). The visible manifestation (Acts 8:18) of the Holy Spirit among the Samaritans does not make them *spiritually* acceptable to God. God had given them eternal life the moment they trusted in the risen Christ to forgive them of their disobedience. The outward display of the Holy Spirit's filling does, however, make them *culturally* acceptable to the Jewish Church, especially since two very respected apostles witness the event.

Meanwhile, God leads Philip to journey south on a road from Jerusalem to Gaza (Acts 8:26). After encountering an Ethiopian eunuch and communicating God's plan of salvation to him (Acts 8:26–39), Philip eventually follows the road system (Acts 8:40) north to the region of Samaria, stopping at the predominantly Gentile city of Caesarea, the Roman capital of Palestine located on the Mediterranean coast. There he continues preaching, but apparently only to Jews and Samaritans, since Peter later comes to Caesarea as the first to preach to Gentiles. Philip's diligent and effective proclamation of the message of Christ in Samaria earns him the title of "Philip the evangelist" (Acts 21:8).

With the Samaritans now significantly evangelized, God prepares to launch **the third advance** of the message of Christ. For this phase of the gospel's expansion, God surprisingly chooses a man named Saul, a fierce persecutor of the Church (Acts 8:3). God takes this self-righteous Pharisee and miraculously changes him into the famous apostle **Paul**, who boldly proclaims the truth of Christ's resurrection to **Gentiles**. The writer of the book of Acts devotes thirteen chapters to this third advance, beginning with the ninth chapter. Let's trace the path of how the nations hear of God's love and forgiveness through the apostle Paul.

Not content to persecute the followers of Christ living in Jerusalem, Saul asks and receives permission from the high priest—still Caiaphas at the time—to travel to Damascus to capture believers and bring them in chains back to Jerusalem for trial (Acts 9:1–2). As he approaches Damascus, located 133 miles north of Jerusalem, the Lord Jesus strikes Saul with a blinding light and instructs him to enter the city and await further instructions (Acts 9:3–9).

At the direction of the Lord, an understandably reluctant disciple named Ananias locates Saul. As Ananias prays for him, Saul receives his sight. It takes only a few days before Saul begins proclaiming Jesus as the Son of God and the promised Messiah in the synagogues of the city (Acts 9:20–22).

What Luke notes as "many days" (Acts 9:23), Saul later clarifies as "three years" (Galatians 1:18). During this time Saul leaves for Arabia where he apparently spends much time studying the Scriptures (Galatians 1:11–17). At some point after Saul returns to Damascus, the Jews plot to kill him, guarding every exit out of the city in order to capture him. Fortunately, the followers of Christ learn of the plot and help Saul sneak out of the city by placing him in a large basket and lowering him over the city wall (Acts 9:23–25). Arriving in Jerusalem, Saul speaks boldly about the Lord Jesus, as he had done in Damascus, causing the Jews to attempt to kill him. Concerned for his safety, the disciples send Saul to Tarsus via Caesarea (Acts 9:26–30).

God has now prepared His chosen leader to proclaim the message of Christ to Gentiles, but before Saul can successfully launch the third advance of the gospel, God must prepare His Church to receive Gentiles. Recall that Jewish believers, because of sinful cultural prejudices, had a difficult time accepting the inclusion of Samaritans into their fellowship. In comparison, accepting Gentiles might prove completely impossible unless the believers see God's stamp of approval on them, just as they had seen God's manifestation of the Spirit's filling of the Samaritans. The strength of their prejudice would also require verification from someone they greatly trusted. Saul, having thrown many of their friends and relatives in jail, certainly lacked the credibility to convince them. Only someone of Peter's stature would suffice. Until the followers of Christ could overcome this significant cultural barrier against Gentiles, their prejudice would limit the message of God's love and forgiveness to only the Jews and Samaritans. This situation sets the context for Acts 10.

The action takes place in Caesarea, located about sixty-five miles northwest of Jerusalem, where the Romans stationed a six-hundred-man Italian cohort. One of the soldiers, a centurion named Cornelius, receives a vision from God (Acts 10:1–6) to send for Peter who is ministering in Joppa, thirty miles to the south (Acts 9:32–43). Cornelius, known by the Jews as a devout God-fearer (someone who worshiped the God of Israel, yet had not converted to Judaism), immediately sends two of his servants and one of his soldiers to find and retrieve Peter (Acts 10:7–8).

While the three emissaries make the two-day trip to Joppa, Peter receives his own divine vision in which God stresses to Peter not to consider anything unholy once God has cleansed it (Acts 10:9–16). The vision doesn't make sense to Peter (Acts 10:17–23) until he follows the three men back to Cornelius' residence in Caesarea. There he finds

Cornelius with his relatives and close friends waiting on him to announce a message from God (Acts 10:24–33).

Suddenly, God's heart for the nations (Acts 10:34–35) becomes clear to Peter, and without hesitation he begins to proclaim how all people can now receive forgiveness because of the resurrection of Jesus Christ (Acts 10:36–43). As Peter preaches God's plan of salvation, the Holy Spirit fills the Gentile gathering in a visible manner, just as He did when the Jews and the Samaritans first received the gospel (Acts 10:44–48). The whole affair amazes the circumcised believers who had accompanied Peter because, in their minds, an uncircumcised Gentile could not become a follower of Christ until the Gentile first became a circumcised Jew.

We would think that the Jewish believers in Jerusalem would rejoice because the event at Cornelius' house began to fulfill in a significant way the theme of the Bible: **God receiving glory by restoring fellowship between all people groups and Himself through Jesus Christ, the Messiah.** Actually, just the opposite happens. Their cultural prejudice against Gentiles blinds them to the heart of God and makes them upset with Peter (Acts 11:1–3). Fortunately, Peter's description of the Holy Spirit filling the Gentiles convinces them that God wants to give eternal life not only to the circumcised Jew but also to the uncircumcised Gentile (Acts 11:15–18).

THE HOLY SPIRIT'S FILLING

ETHNIC GROUP	PASSAGE	APOSTLE
Jews	Acts 2:4	Peter
Samaritans	Acts 8:14–17	Peter
Gentiles	Acts 10:44–47	Peter

God's chosen leader stands ready—Saul, who becomes the future apostle Paul. God has now also corrected the sinful prejudicial attitude of

Jewish and Samaritan believers so that they can receive Gentiles into their fellowship in the Church. Only one preparation remains before launching the third advance of the gospel: a launching pad for the apostle Paul, or rather a local church to send him out to the nations. Let's see how God puts all this together.

When Christ's followers finally realize that Gentiles could receive God's love and forgiveness without first becoming converts to Judaism, it doesn't take long before the believers begin intentionally proclaiming the message of Christ to the uncircumcised. Soon a large number of Gentiles in Antioch—the capital of Syria located three hundred miles north from Jerusalem—turns to the Lord (Acts 11:19–21). As the number of believers grows in Antioch, the apostles in Jerusalem send Barnabas, and there he encourages even more Gentiles to come to faith in Christ (Acts 11:22–24). With the Antioch church rapidly growing, Barnabas then travels one hundred miles to Tarsus to recruit Saul (Paul) to help him with all the new believers—now called "Christians" by the people of Antioch (Acts 11:25–26).

After a couple of years the church in Antioch grows strong enough to make a bold move. The leadership of the Antioch church, guided by the Spirit, decides to send Barnabas and Saul on a mission trip to proclaim the message of God's love and forgiveness to other Gentiles (Acts 13:1–3). The third advance of the gospel now moves from the preparation phase to the full implementation phase. At this point, Saul takes responsibility as the leader of the mission and begins to go by his Roman name, Paul.

ADVANCE	#1	#2	#3
LEADER	Peter	Philip	Paul
CULTURAL GROUP	Jews	Samaritans	Gentiles
SCRIPTURE	Acts 2–7	Acts 8	Acts 9–21

Leaving Antioch via the port city of Seleucia, the *first missionary journey* begins on the island of Cyprus, Barnabas' birthplace. John Mark, the future author of the Gospel of Mark, joins them during this part of their mission (Acts 13:4–13). Sailing to Asia Minor—modern-day Turkey—Paul and Barnabas start churches in the Galatian cities of Antioch (different from the Antioch they left in Syria), Iconium, Lystra, and Derbe (Acts 13:14–14:26). Later Paul writes his epistle of Galatians to the Christians in these cities. Returning home from their trip, they report to their sending church how God had opened a door of faith to the Gentiles (Acts 14:27).

While Paul and Barnabas furlough in Antioch, Syria, a group of men known as Judaizers arrive from Judea and begin to teach that Gentiles cannot receive forgiveness for their sins without first being circumcised (Acts 15:1). The controversy requires Paul and Barnabas to travel to Jerusalem to settle the issue with the apostles and elders (Acts 15:2–6). During the debate Peter reminds the heated gathering that God had given the Holy Spirit to Gentile believers in the same way He had to Jewish believers. Peter concludes that God grants salvation to both Jew and Gentile because of His grace, not because either observed the Law of Moses (Acts 15:7–11). James, the half-brother of Jesus, officially settles the dispute in favor of Paul and Barnabas (Acts 15:12–35). The false teaching of the Judaizers, however, does not stop, but continues to plague the Church.

Not long after returning to Antioch in Syria, Paul and Barnabas decide to return to the cities of Galatia to check on the churches they previously started (Acts 15:36). Unfortunately, a dispute over whether to take John Mark with them causes a split between Barnabas, who wanted to take John Mark, and Paul, who refused to do so because John Mark had deserted them after their ministry in Cyprus. The disagreement results in Barnabas taking his cousin (Colossians 4:10) with him to minister in

Cyprus and Paul taking a man named Silas, a participant at the Jerusalem Council, with him to Galatia (Acts 15:37–41).

When Paul and Silas make this *second missionary journey,* they first visit the Galatian Christians and deliver the decree established by the apostles and elders at the Jerusalem Council, explaining unequivocally that Gentiles did not need to become converts to Judaism before receiving God's love and forgiveness. Their ministry strengthens the faith and increases the number of new believers in the Gentile churches (Acts 16:1–5).

Completing their work among the Galatian churches, the missionary team of Paul and Silas as well as a young believer named Timothy (who joined them at the city of Lystra) continues their journey in what we know as the country of Turkey. They want to take the message of Christ to the region of Bithynia located north of Galatia, but God directs them to go preach the gospel in the region of Macedonia, which we know as the northern portion of modern-day Greece (Acts 16:6–10).

Setting sail from Troas where they add Luke the physician to their missionary band (Acts 16:11), they soon arrive in Philippi. Paul's ministry in Philippi has both positive and negative results. Two households—those of Lydia and of a jailor, together with their families—cross over into a right relationship with God. Yet Paul endures a beating and time in jail as a result of casting out a demon from a woman (Acts 16:12–40). Later Paul writes his letter of Philippians to the church he helps start in this city.

After leaving Luke in Philippi (Acts 17:1), the team moves on to the city of Thessalonica. Paul proclaims Christ's suffering and resurrection, resulting in a great multitude responding to the message of forgiveness (Acts 17:1–4). Again, everything does not work out favorably, because his preaching causes such a riot that Paul decides to move on to the next city (Acts 17:5–9). Paul eventually writes two letters to the church he leaves behind, the epistles of 1 and 2 Thessalonians.

The missionary team arrives next at Berea, where many believe the good news and receive the free gift of eternal life (Acts 17:10–12). You can probably guess what happens next: another riot. So Paul leaves Silas and Timothy in Berea and travels to Athens (Acts 17:13–15).

In Athens, as Paul waits on Silas and Timothy to rejoin him, he preaches about Jesus both in the synagogue and in the marketplace. Eventually, some Epicureans (philosophers who focus on pleasure) and Stoics (philosophers who focus on pain) hear him and take him before the Areopagus—a council of influential Athenians who originally met on a hill dedicated to Mars, the Roman god of war (Acts 17:16–21). There, Paul contextualizes his message for his Greek audience, using their altar dedicated to an unknown god to segue into the resurrection of Jesus Christ. Paul's declaration receives a varied response. Some sneer, some insist on hearing more about the resurrection, and some believe in Christ as their Savior (Acts 17:22–34).

Paul journeys next to the Greek city of Corinth (Acts 18:1), where he ministers with Aquila and Priscilla (Acts 18:2–3) and reconnects with Silas and Timothy (Acts 18:5). Many Corinthians believe as he proclaims Jesus as the Christ (Acts 18:8), and to these believers he later writes the letters of 1 and 2 Corinthians. After a year and a half (Acts 18:11), Paul returns to Antioch for another furlough (Acts 18:22).

MISSIONARY TRIP	SCRIPTURE	PRIMARY DESTINATION	MAIN TEAMMATES
First	Acts 13:4–14:28	Modern-day Turkey	Barnabas, John Mark
Second	Acts 15:36–18:22	Modern-day Greece	Silas, Timothy, Luke
Third	Acts 18:23–21:16	Modern-day Turkey	Timothy, Luke, Aquila, Priscilla, Titus (2 Cor. 8:6)

After some time in Antioch, Paul begins his *third missionary journey*. He begins this trip as he did his second trip, by visiting the Galatians to strengthen their faith (Acts 18:23). He then travels to Ephesus, a city he had briefly visited on his second missionary journey (Acts 19:1). God gives Paul a fruitful ministry, for all who live in Asia, the western province of Asia Minor, hear the word of the Lord (Acts 19:10). Considerable numbers turn away from worshiping Artemis (Acts 19:23–26), the Greek goddess of fertility whose temple in Ephesus became known as one of the seven wonders of the ancient world. Paul stays in Ephesus for three years (Acts 20:31) before persecution (Acts 19:27–29) causes him to leave (Acts 20:1). He later writes the New Testament book called Ephesians to the believers in this city.

From Ephesus, Paul visits the churches in Macedonia that he started on his second missionary journey and reunites with Luke at Philippi where Paul had left him on the second mission trip (Acts 20:6). Three months later, he begins his return trip home intending first to visit Jerusalem, if possible, on the day of Pentecost (Acts 20:16), even though other believers warned of trials that await him (Acts 21:10–16).

As a result of these three gospel advances, the message of God's love and forgiveness spreads throughout the Roman Empire. Peter's four sermons take the message of Christ first to Jews. Philip's bold move to explain the resurrection to Samaritans advances faith in the Messiah across a huge cultural divide. The great apostle Paul's three missionary journeys saturate the modern-day countries of Turkey and Greece, filling many new churches with believing Gentiles. During the Public Period, the Church expands greatly as it proclaims the message of forgiveness through faith in the risen Jesus Christ. The arrival of Paul in Jerusalem, however, marks a transition for the Church. It moves from its Public Period to its Trials Period, a time of great suffering and persecution of the Church that we will consider in the next chapter.

Now let's gain a better understanding of where the three advances occur geographically.

WHERE?

The Church's message of Christ's love and forgiveness moves into the world by advancing through concentric circles, representing greater to lesser degrees of Jewish cultural influence. While doing so, it follows the geographical map that the Lord Jesus highlighted in Acts 1:8 when He said, "But you shall receive power when the Holy Spirit has come upon you; and you shall be My witnesses both in Jerusalem, and in all Judea and Samaria, and even to the remotest part of the earth." Using this verse as a guide, we can trace where the events occur in the Public Period of the Church.

LOCATION	LEADER	ADVANCE	SCRIPTURE
In Jerusalem	Peter	To Jews	Acts 2–7
In all Judea and Samaria	Philip	To Samaritans	Acts 8
Even to the remotest part of the earth	Paul	To Gentiles	Acts 9–21

Peter Takes the Gospel to the Jews in Jerusalem

The events of Acts 2–7 take place during the gospel's first advance under Peter's leadership in Jerusalem. Two places in particular stand out: the upper room (1) and the temple (2).

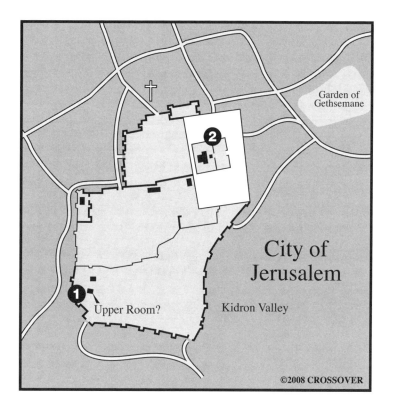

Philip Takes the Gospel to the Samaritans in Samaria

The events of Acts 8 focused on the message of Christ going to all Judea and Samaria under Philip's leadership. This second advance focuses primarily on Samaria, since Luke devotes only a phrase (Acts 8:1) to what occurs in Judea. The action begins in a city of the region of Samaria. Scholars debate whether this city represents the city actually named Samaria (1a), which served as the capital of the Northern Kingdom during the Divided Era of the Old Testament but, at this point, contains mostly Gentile residents; or the city of Shechem (1b), which during this time serves as the religious center of the Samaritans. Philip's evangelistic encounter with the Ethiopian eunuch occurs on the road (2) from Jerusalem to Gaza. Ethiopia (3) refers not the modern-day country of Ethiopia but to ancient Nubia, located according to today's maps between southern Egypt and northern Sudan. As Philip travels north along the coast he ministers in various cities, of which Scripture mentions the ancient Philistine city of Azotus (4), until he reaches the Samaritan city of Caesarea (5), located sixty-five miles northwest of Jerusalem.

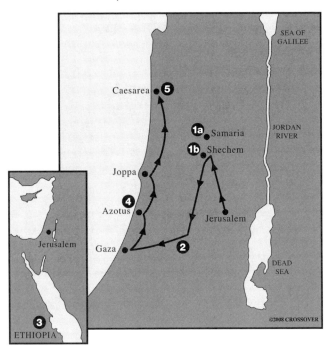

God's Preparation of Paul

Before the third advance could launch the good news to the Gentiles living in the remotest part of the earth, God has to prepare His messenger and His Church. Luke describes this preparation in the events of Acts

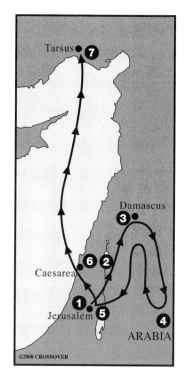

9–11. In Acts 9 Paul leaves Jerusalem (1) in order to persecute Christians in Damascus, which today stands as the oldest continually inhabited city in the world. While traveling on the road (2) to Damascus, he meets the Lord Jesus. After spending time in Damascus (3) and Arabia (4), he travels to Jerusalem (5) where Barnabas meets him and introduces him to the apostles. An attempt on his life causes him to travel via Caesarea (6) to Tarsus (7), the capital of Cilicia.

God's Preparation of His Church

With the future leader of the third advance prepared, attention turns to the preparation of God's Church in which the Lord needed to overcome sinful cultural prejudice against Gentiles. After Paul leaves for Tarsus in Acts 9, the rest of the chapter describes Peter following a path along the Mediterranean coast similar to that of Philip's ministry above. Peter ministers first in Lydda (1) and then in Joppa (2). While Peter ministers in Joppa, the action moves to Acts 10. God directs Cornelius, who lives in the city of Caesarea (3), to send for Peter in Joppa, thirty miles to the south. When Peter arrives he preaches to Cornelius' Gentile relatives and close friends, with many coming to Christ. Moving on to Acts 11, we find Peter arriving back in Jerusalem (4), where the apostles demand an explanation of his visit to the unclean Gentiles. His description of how the Holy Spirit fell on the Gentiles as He had fallen on the disciples at Pentecost opens their eyes to God's heart for all nations. It does not take long before the circumcised believers begin to proclaim the message of God's love and forgiveness to the uncircumcised and unbelieving Gentiles in the city of Antioch (5), the third largest city in the Roman Empire. **Antioch** soon becomes the center of the Church's missionary outreach, qualifying it as the key city of the Church's Public Period.

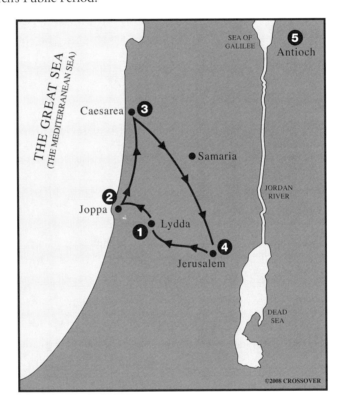

Paul's First Missionary Journey

At Antioch (1), in the Roman province of Syria, God's great plan for the Church taking the gospel to the remotest part of the earth begins to come together. With His messenger and Church prepared, the Holy

Spirit sends Paul and Barnabas on their first missionary journey, which Luke records in Acts 13–14. The ministry team travels on land to the port of Seleucia (2) and then sails to the port of Salamis (3), situated on the east coast of Cyprus and the largest city on the island. They travel the ninety miles across this Roman province to the capital city of Paphos (4). From this port they sail to Perga (5), the capital of the Roman province of Pamphylia, located on the southern coast of Asia Minor. Traveling on land, they arrive in the Roman province of Galatia. There they proclaim the resurrection of the Lord Jesus Christ throughout the cities of Antioch (6) in the district of Pisidia as well as Iconium (7), Lystra (8), and Derbe (9), all in the district of Lycaonia. Paul and Barnabas return to Perga and sail from the port city of Attalia (10). They end their trip where they started it, in the Syrian city of Antioch (1).

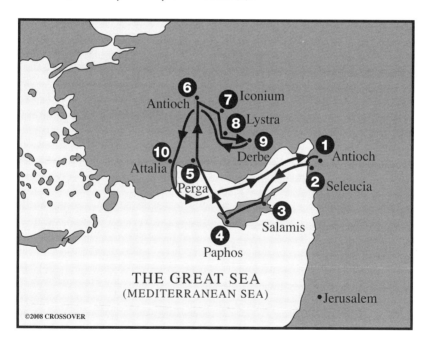

Paul's Second Missionary Journey

At the end of Acts 15—after attending the Church council in Jerusalem where the apostles officially decide that Gentiles do not have to convert to Judaism before or after coming to Christ—Paul begins his second missionary journey from the Syrian Antioch (1), taking Silas instead of Barnabas. They first visit churches throughout the province of Syria (2) and in the district of Cilicia (3). In Acts 16, after visiting the Galatian churches in the cities of Derbe (4) and Lystra (5), they add Timothy to their team and continue their journey through Phrygia (6), a region overlapping the Roman provinces of Galatia and Asia. Reaching a region in the northern portion of Asia called Mysia (7), they want to go to Bithynia (8), but the Spirit directs them to Troas (9), a major seaport on the northwest shore of Asia Minor in the Roman province of Asia, where Luke probably joins them.

A vision motivates Paul and his missionary team to sail to Samothrace (10), a small mountainous island, and then to Neapolis (11), a port in the Roman province of Macedonia. From there they travel ten miles by land to the city of Philippi (12), where they plant the first church on the continent of Europe. Leaving Luke in Philippi, the rest of the team travels along the great Roman road known as the Via Egnatia through the cities of Amphipolis (13) and Apollonia (14), stopping at Thessalonica (15) at the foot of Mount Olympus, where the Greek gods supposedly lived. In Thessalonica Paul and his team plant another church before trouble with local Jews forces them to move on to Berea (16).

Though the Bereans eagerly receive the apostle's message, the Thessalonian Jews who follow Paul to Berea force him to leave. He travels twenty-four miles to the coast of the Aegean Sea where he takes a boat to Athens (17), the most famous of the Greek cities, located in the Roman province of Achaia. By Acts 18 we find Paul leaving Athens and traveling forty-eight miles west to Corinth (18), the capital city of Achaia.

From Corinth the apostle Paul begins his journey home. He sails from Cenchrea (19), the eastern port of Corinth situated about eight miles east of the city, to the western shore of Asia Minor where he ports at Ephesus (20), the most important city of the Roman province of Asia. From Ephesus he sails about five hundred miles to Caesarea (21), where he travels sixty-five miles southeast to Jerusalem (22). After visiting the believers in that city, he returns to Antioch (23) in Syria.

Paul's Third Missionary Journey

Soon Paul leaves Antioch (1) on his third missionary journey. He first visits churches both in the Roman province of Galatia (2) and in the region called Phrygia, (3) where he strengthens all the disciples. In Acts 19 we find the apostle Paul arriving in Ephesus (4) in the Roman province of Asia—not to be confused with the modern-day continent of Asia. Acts 20 describes Paul leaving Ephesus after a riot and going to the Roman province of Macedonia (5). After passing through Macedonia he travels to the Roman province of Achaia (6). Returning to Macedonia (7) he picks up Luke in Philippi (8) and they sail to Troas (9). From Troas he travels twenty miles by land without his team to Assos (10) and then by sea with his team to the port of Mitylene (11). From Mitylene, they sail to the islands of Chios (12) and Samos (13) before porting at Miletus (14) in the Roman province of Asia, thirty-plus miles south of Ephesus. In Acts 21, Paul and his companions sail from Miletus to the mountain-ous Aegean island of Cos (15), then to the 46-by-18-mile-long island of Rhodes (16) off the southwest coast of Asia Minor, and then to the port of Patara (17) located on the coast of Lycia, a small Roman province in Asia Minor. From Patara they sail four hundred miles past the southern coast of Cyprus to the Phoenician city of Tyre (18). After the ship un-loads its cargo the team continues by sea another twenty miles south to

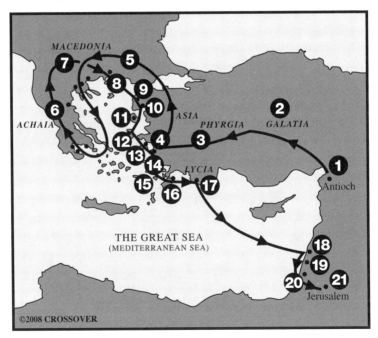

PUTTING TOGETHER THE PUZZLE OF THE NEW TESTAMENT

Ptolemais (19) in the district of Galilee. From there they travel either by land or sea another forty miles to Caesarea (20). After the missionary team spends time with Philip—the deacon turned evangelist—they finish their journey by traveling the sixty-five miles to Jerusalem (21).

We move now to identify the approximate dates for each of the gospel's advances to the three cultural groups of people: Jews, Samaritans, and Gentiles.

WHEN?

We have two tasks before us. First, we must identify the beginning and ending dates of the Church's Public Period. Second, we must seek to determine what years the three gospel advances occurred as well as other major events within this historical time period. Please understand the attitude of humility with which we approach this search. Though we can confirm many of the following dates from reliable historical data, others we must infer. So unless we have absolute certainty, we must add our key word *approximately* to every date in this section.

Let's work on identifying the beginning and ending dates of the Church's Public Period. We know that this period begins in Jerusalem on the day of Pentecost in AD 30. We also know this period ends in Jerusalem sometime around Pentecost, because Acts 20:16 notes that Paul, returning from his third missionary journey, decides to hurriedly sail past Ephesus in order to arrive in Jerusalem, if possible, in time to celebrate the feast. To determine how many years passed between these two feasts of Pentecost, we must once again do some detective work.

The best clues come from Acts 24:27. This verse provides two key pieces of evidence: (1) Paul resided in jail for two years after arriving in Jerusalem around Pentecost, and (2) Festus succeeded Felix as governor of Palestine. If we know the date Festus became governor, we can determine the ending date by subtracting two years. Most historians point to AD 59 as the date when the transition occurred, making AD 57 the ending date of this time period. So the entire period lasts **twenty-seven years**.

Now we must seek to determine the dates of the three gospel advances as well as other major events during the Church's Public Period. History provides us with several significant markers. We know from external sources that the death of King Herod Agrippa (grandson of Herod the Great), recorded in Acts 12:23, occurred in AD 44.

Regarding Paul's second missionary journey, we also know that Gallio, the proconsul mentioned in Acts 18:12, governs in Achaia around AD 51–52, which pinpoints the eighteen months when Paul ministers in Corinth at the end of his second missionary journey. We find an additional clue in Acts 18:2, which describes Emperor Claudius commanding the Jews to leave Rome. We know from history that this decree occurs in AD 49.

Other key verses denote the amount of time the apostle Paul spends in various locations during his third missionary journey. He spends at least three months in Greece (Acts 20:2–3) and three years in Ephesus (Acts 20:31) in addition to the time spent in extensive travel to other places of ministry. If we subtract this amount of time from the AD 57 Pentecost at the end of his trip, then Paul's third missionary journey begins around AD 53 at the latest.

TIMETABLE FOR PUBLIC PERIOD OF THE CHURCH

Beginning date	Pentecost, May AD 30	(Acts 2:5)
Gospel advances to Jews	AD 30	Acts 2–7
Gospel advances to Samaritans	AD 31	Acts 8
Conversion of the apostle Paul	AD 32	Acts 9
Paul's first visit to Jerusalem	AD 35	Acts 9
Gospel advances to Gentiles	≈ AD 37–38	Acts 10–11
Herod Agrippa dies	AD 44	Acts 12
First missionary journey	AD 46–48	Acts 13–14
Jerusalem Council	AD 49	Acts 15
Second missionary journey	AD 50–52	Acts 16–18
Third missionary journey	AD 53–57	Acts 19–21
Ending date	Pentecost, May AD 57	(Acts 20:16)

For various reasons, most biblical scholars place the Church council in Jerusalem of Acts 15 taking place in AD 49, which seems appropriate, since Paul left on his second missionary journey from Antioch soon after attending the council. Using this date, we can determine the approximate time of Paul's Damascus-road conversion. We subtract the three years mentioned in Galatians 1:18—which describes the time between his conversion (Galatians 1:15–17) and his first trip to Jerusalem to meet Peter (Cephas) and James the Lord's brother—as well as subtract the fourteen years mentioned in Galatians 2:1, which refers to his trip to the Jerusalem Council. Together, these two time periods (three years plus fourteen years) equal seventeen years between his conversion and the

Jerusalem Council. This information places AD 32 as the approximate time of Paul's conversion, or two years after the resurrection.

We know that the gospel advances to the Jews immediately on the day of the first Pentecost in AD 30 and to the Samaritans before the apostle Paul's conversion on the road to Damascus in AD 32.

Pinpointing the first missionary journey makes for a difficult task. We at least know it occurs between the death of Herod (AD 44) and the Jerusalem Council (AD 49). The only clues that provide any insight into length of time come from Acts 14:3 and Acts 14:28. In both verses Luke writes that Paul and Barnabas spend "a long time" during their first missionary journey in Iconium before traveling to Lystra, and they spend "a long time" in Antioch before going to Jerusalem to participate in the council in AD 49. Granted, these clues do not give much specificity, but these hints added to other more technical markers nudge many historians to approximate the first missionary journey somewhere in the range of AD 46 to AD 48.

One last entry remains for us to add to our timetable. Approximately when did the gospel begin its advance among the Gentiles in Acts 10? We know that it occurs after Paul first visits Jerusalem (Acts 9:26–27), which we know from Galatians 1:18 happens three years after his conversion in AD 32. So the message of Christ advances to the Gentiles no sooner than AD 35. We also know that the advance must have occurred before the AD 44 death of Herod in Acts 12. But how much before? Acts 11:25–26 tells us that Paul (Saul) spends an entire year teaching in Antioch, Syria, after Barnabas recruits him from Tarsus. If we subtract the time Barnabas ministered in Antioch before retrieving Paul, we can conclude that AD 42 marks the absolute latest date for the events of Acts 10 and 11 to have occurred. Therefore, Peter seems to have advanced the gospel to the Gentile Cornelius somewhere between AD 36 and AD 42—granted, a very large window of time. Many historians' estimate hovers around the AD 37 or AD 38 range.

Though we can verify some of these dates with historical data of events independent of Scripture—as in the death of Herod Agrippa, the reign of Claudius, and the administrations of Gallio, Felix, and Festus— we must admit that, until we obtain more evidence from archeology or from historical documents, several of these dates remain educated guesses. Therefore, remember our key word: *approximately*. This section benefits us, however, by providing a general idea of when the events of the Church's Public Period occur. We do know that the entire period extends from Pentecost AD 30 to Pentecost AD 57, a span of twenty-seven years.

WHY?

If the Old Testament *promised* the Messiah and the Gospels *provided* Him, in the book of Acts the Church *proclaimed* Him. Though the Going of the Church Era begins with the Church patiently waiting for the Holy Spirit to prepare them, it does not take long before they take the message of Christ to the nations. After the Holy Spirit fills them with power, they immediately get to work advancing the good news of eternal life through faith in Jesus Christ.

During the twenty-seven years of the Public Period, the growth of the Church reaches astounding proportions. The Spirit-filled followers of Christ not only establish churches in many provinces of the Roman Empire but the Church also grows from 120 believers gathered in an up- per room to thousands of believers scattered around the Mediterranean as the following chart demonstrates.

GROWTH OF THE CHURCH DURING THE PUBLIC PERIOD

Acts 2:41	"There were added that day about three thousand souls."
Acts 2:47	"And the Lord was adding to their number day by day those who were being saved."
Acts 4:4	"Many of those who had heard the message believed; and the number of the men came to be about five thousand."
Acts 5:14	"And all the more believers in the Lord, multitudes of men and women, were constantly added to their number."
Acts 6:7	"And the number of the disciples continued to increase greatly in Jerusalem, and a great many of the priests were becoming obedient to the faith."
Acts 8:12	"But when they believed Philip preaching the good news about the kingdom of God and the name of Jesus Christ, they were being baptized, men and women alike."
Acts 9:31	"So the church throughout all Judea and Galilee and Samaria enjoyed peace, being built up; and, going on in the fear of the Lord and in the comfort of the Holy Spirit, it continued to increase."
Acts 9:35	"And all who lived at Lydda and Sharon saw him, and they turned to the Lord."
Acts 9:42	"And it became known all over Joppa, and many believed in the Lord."
Acts 11:21	"And the hand of the Lord was with them, and a large number who believed turned to the Lord."
Acts 12:24	"But the word of the Lord continued to grow and to be multiplied."
Acts 13:48	"And when the Gentiles heard this, . . . as many as had been appointed to eternal life believed."
Acts 14:1	"A great multitude believed, both of Jews and of Greeks."
Acts 14:21	"After they had preached the gospel to that city and had made many disciples."
Acts 16:5	"And were increasing in number daily."
Acts 17:4	"And some of them were persuaded and joined Paul and Silas, along with a great multitude of the God-fearing Greeks and a number of the leading women."
Acts 17:12	"Many of them therefore believed, along with a number of prominent Greek women and men."
Acts 17:34	"Some men joined him and believed."
Acts 18:8	"Many of the Corinthians when they heard were believing and being baptized."
Acts 19:20	"So the word of the Lord was growing mightily and prevailing."

So in three strategic advances the overall theme of the Bible comes clearly into focus: **God receiving glory by restoring fellowship between the nations and Himself through His Son, Jesus Christ.** Though most students of the Bible know that the book of Acts stresses the Church taking the message of Christ to the nations, many do not realize that the letters of Paul also stress the same theme. Many mistakenly think that the Epistles focus strictly on what Christians should believe and how they should live. Not so! In fact, it should not surprise us that the Epistles also deal with God's heart for the nations, because the apostle Paul writes most of his epistles as follow-up letters to the churches he had planted on his missionary journeys.

Not only does the Bible provide the basis for mission work but mission work also provides the basis for the Bible. Selecting just a few of many possible verses, let's see how Paul's epistles continue to stress the theme of God reconciling all people groups to Himself through His Son, Jesus Christ. Note the emphasized phrases in the following verses.

- **Paul's First Missionary Journey:** "Seeing that I had been *entrusted with the gospel to the uncircumcised*, just as Peter had been to the circumcised" (Galatians 2:7).
- **Paul's Second Missionary Journey:** "Hindering us from *speaking to the Gentiles that they might be saved*" (1 Thessalonians 2:16); "And it was for this *He called you through our gospel*, that you may gain the glory of Lord Jesus Christ" (2 Thessalonians 2:14). In this verse, *you* refers to Gentile Thessalonians.
- **Paul's Third Missionary Journey:** "Thus, for my part, I am eager to preach the gospel to you also who are in Rome. For I am not ashamed of *the gospel, for it is the power of God for salvation to everyone who believes, to the Jew first and also to the Greek*" (Romans 1:15–16); "And to the Jews I became as a Jew, that I might win Jews; to those who are under the Law,

as under the Law, though not being myself under the Law, *that I might win those who are under the Law*; to those who are without law, as without law, though not being without the law of God but under the law of Christ, *that I might win those who are without law*. To the weak I became weak, that I might win the weak; I have become all things to all men, *that I may by all means save some. And I do all things for the sake of the gospel*, that I may become a fellow partaker of it" (1 Corinthians 9:20–23);

- "So as to *preach the gospel even to the regions beyond you*, and not to boast in what has been accomplished in the sphere of another" (2 Corinthians 10:16).

Having seen the tremendous emphasis Paul's epistles place on the Church's proclamation of the message of Christ for the nations to experience reconciliation with God, let's look more closely at Paul to see what we can learn about him.

WHO?

The apostle Paul represents our sixth New Testament author. We can easily remember the first four writers because the first four New Testament books, the Gospels, bear their names: Matthew, Mark, Luke, and John. We can remember the next two authors, Peter and now Paul, when we realize that the first half of the book of Acts (chapters 1–12) focuses primarily on Peter's leadership and the second half of Acts (chapters 13–28) concentrates primarily on Paul's leadership.

The New Testament provides many details about the apostle Paul, some of which we've already covered in the sections above, particularly the How? section. The next chapter on the Trials Period of the Church will give us even more details. For this reason, let's limit ourselves here to gaining an overview of the spiritual journey he followed as God changed him from Saul, the persecutor of Christians, to Paul, the planter of churches. Four passages of Scripture guide our investigation: two about his life before he meets Christ, one on how he meets Christ, and one on his life after he meets Christ.

In just two short passages, Acts 22:3 and Philippians 3:5–6, we discover much about Paul's life before he meets Christ. His Jewish parents, who traced their lineage to the tribe of Benjamin, have him circumcised on the eighth day after his birth in Tarsus, Cilicia. As an adult, Paul (Saul) becomes a Pharisee after the famous rabbi Gamaliel educates him in Jerusalem. After watching the stoning of Stephen (Acts 7:58), he persecutes believers by forcibly dragging them to prison.

Acts 9 graphically describes Paul's conversion. On his way to persecute believers in Damascus, a flash of heavenly light blinds him. Falling to the ground, he hears the Lord Jesus speak to him. His companions lead him by the hand into the city, where he spends three days neither eating nor drinking, until Ananias finds him. After Ananias prays for him, Saul (Paul) receives his sight and Ananias baptizes him.

PAUL'S SPIRITUAL JOURNEY

Before meeting Christ	Acts 22:3 Phil. 3:5–6	Born in Tarsus of Cilicia Born Jewish Circumcised the eighth day Grows up in Jerusalem Educated under Gamaliel Becomes a Pharisee Persecutes the Church
While meeting Christ	Acts 9:1–18	Blinded by a heavenly light Hears the Lord Jesus speak to him Enters Damascus Waits three days without eating or drinking Meets Ananias who prays for him Receives his sight Baptized by Ananias
After meeting Christ	2 Cor. 11:24–28	Receives thirty-nine lashes five times Beaten with rods three times Stoned with rocks one time Shipwrecked three times Spends a day and a night in the ocean Exposed to constant danger Experiences hunger and thirst Exposed to cold weather Burdened by concerns for churches

We already know the impact Paul's church-planting activities exerts on the spread of the gospel among the Gentiles, but what kind of price did he pay during this third advance of Christianity? In 2 Corinthians 11:24–28 Paul vividly recounts the external and internal costs of his missionary activity. Five times the Jewish people give him thirty-nine lashes. Three times he receives beatings with rods and once a pelting with rocks. Three ships on which he sailed wreck, and one of those times he spends a day and a night in the ocean, either swimming or perhaps in a small boat, until someone rescues him. Traveling constantly exposes him to a variety of dangers including surviving in the wilderness and avoiding thieves. Additionally, he knows the pain of hunger, thirst, and cold weather. Even in safe and comfortable surroundings, he still carries the inner burden of concern for the purity and protection of the fledgling churches he has planted. Definitely not the life he envisioned for himself as he traveled the road to Damascus.

In the midst of such an incredible life, the apostle Paul finds time to write half of the books in the New Testament. We know he writes at least thirteen books, and, if he wrote the book of Hebrews, the total reaches fourteen. The following chart, which excludes the book of Hebrews, shows when he wrote each of the thirteen epistles.

THE WRITINGS OF THE APOSTLE PAUL

WHEN	WHAT
Written after his first missionary journey	Galatians
Written during his second missionary journey	1 Thessalonians 2 Thessalonians
Written during his third missionary journey	Romans 1 Corinthians 2 Corinthians
Written during his first Roman imprisonment	Ephesians Philippians Colossians Philemon
Written during his release from prison	1 Timothy Titus
Written during his second Roman imprisonment	2 Timothy

FOR NEXT TIME

If you are having an extremely busy week:	If you have a little extra time:	If you can't get enough:
read Acts 21–28.	add Ephesians, Philippians, Colossians, and James.	add 1 Timothy, 2 Timothy, Titus, and Philemon.

PERIOD #7

PERIOD #7

The Church's Trials Period

Though the Coming of the Church Era starts slowly and quietly in its Private Period, the Church explodes onto the world's scene during its Public Period as we saw in the last chapter. In only twenty-seven years we find the Church established throughout much of the Roman Empire. The Church spreads not just geographically but also culturally as it embraces all people groups from Jews in Jerusalem to Gentiles living at the ends of the earth. In three strategic advances led by three powerful leaders, the message of God's love and forgiveness goes forward as believers filled with the Spirit of God proclaim Christ's crucifixion on the cross and resurrection from the dead.

In order to keep the New Testament puzzle clearly in mind, let's review the border once again. If you've diligently reviewed the big picture each chapter, you should not find much difficulty filling in the chart below.

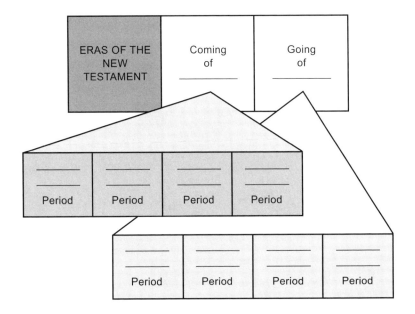

The following chart forms the crux of the New Testament puzzle. The total number of key items from all eight periods eventually reaches forty. The Coming of Christ Era contains twenty-four of the key items, and the Going of the Church Era contains another sixteen key items. If we can articulate in order all forty key items, then we can thoroughly communicate the historical flow of the New Testament. So please don't skip this next review chart. Repetition burns the information deeply into our memories.

CHRIST'S _____ PERIOD: 7 GROUPS	CHRIST'S _____ PERIOD: 7 THEMES	CHRIST'S _____ PERIOD: 7 DAYS
Born to _____ and _____	Inspires the _____	_____ occurs on Sunday
Worshiped by _____	Instructs the _____	_____ occurs on Monday
Honored by _____ and _____	Infuriates the _____	_____ occurs on Tuesday
Sought by _____ and _____	Causes _____	_____ occurs on Wednesday
Taught by temple _____	Cures the _____	_____ and _____ occur on Thursday
Baptized by _____	Casts out _____	_____ occurs on Friday
Tempted by _____	Reveals that we can be _____	_____ occurs on Saturday

CHRIST'S _____ PERIOD: 3 CONFIDENCE BUILDERS	CHURCH'S _____ PERIOD: 3 EVENTS	CHURCH'S _____ PERIOD: 3 ADVANCES
_____	_____	By _____ to the _____
_____	_____	By _____ to the _____
_____	_____	By _____ to the _____

The Public Period of the Church comes to a close as Paul arrives in the city of Jerusalem, ending his third missionary journey. For the remainder of the book of Acts, Paul is imprisoned, thus beginning the Trials Period of the Church. Let's see what happens during this period.

WHAT?

In the first twenty-one chapters of the book of Acts, three men—Peter, Philip, and Paul—advance the message of Christ both culturally and geographically until they have spread Christianity throughout the Roman Empire. Though persecution occurs during the Public Period of the Church, with the exception of Herod Agrippa using a sword to kill James the brother of the apostle John, the affliction suffered by believers as recorded in the book of Acts seems infrequent and limited to short stints in jail, stonings, and beatings. Although not a routine you wake up each morning wanting to experience, the persecution comes nowhere close to the level of affliction the Church suffers during this new period. Because the extent of the **persecution of the Church** increases both in frequency and in intensity, we call this time of New Testament history the Trials Period of the Church.

This third period of the Coming of the Church Era includes not only the final chapters in the book of Acts but also information from epistles that Paul writes during and after prison as well as Peter's two epistles.

THE CHURCH'S TRIALS PERIOD

Acts 21:27–28:31, plus

Ephesians, Philippians, Colossians, Philemon, 1 and 2 Timothy, Titus, and 1 and 2 Peter

Watch closely as we see how the Church not only suffers persecution but also how it victoriously responds to its affliction.

HOW?

Many followers of Christ suffer during the Trials Period of the Church. The Bible, primarily because of Luke's record in the book of Acts, contains much more information about the suffering of the apostle

Paul than of anyone else. Since the vast majority of our information about this period of New Testament history focuses on Paul, we will organize the information around his **three imprisonments.** Let's follow the events that occur during the Trials Period.

In the last chapter we left Paul in Jerusalem, having just finished his third missionary journey in which he proclaimed, for three years, the message of the Messiah to the people of Ephesus. Let's pick up the story in Acts 21:17.

After Paul and his missionary team arrive in Jerusalem, the Christians gladly receive them. The next day Paul meets with James, the half-brother of Jesus and leader of the church in Jerusalem. After Paul relates in detail all that God accomplished among the Gentiles through his ministry, James points out how many thousands of Jews in Jerusalem had placed their faith in the Lord Jesus. James also explains that the believers in Jerusalem zealously follow the Law of Moses, meaning that the Jewish Christians of Jerusalem also strongly believe that genuine salvation does not exempt anyone from observing all the Old Testament laws (Acts 21:17–20).

Out of concern for what these Judaizers might do to Paul when they discover him in Jerusalem, the Church leaders counsel him to demonstrate publicly his cultural commitment to the Law of Moses by paying for the sacrifices that four other believers would offer in the temple (see Numbers 6:13–20). This request poses no problem for Paul. Though he teaches that faith in Christ does not require the Gentiles to *adopt* Jewish culture, he also knows faith in Christ does not require a Jewish person to *forsake* Jewish culture (Acts 21:21–25).

Unfortunately, the plan backfires. A week later, some of the unbelieving Jews from Ephesus who had traveled to Jerusalem to celebrate the feast of Pentecost recognize Paul in the temple. A riot breaks out as they seek to kill the great missionary. News of the ensuing chaos reaches Claudius Lysias, commander of the Roman cohort, who takes some soldiers and centurions with him to intervene (Acts 21:26–31). Entering the turmoil, the soldiers chain Paul and literally carry him to their barracks because of the violence of the mob. Before going inside the barracks, Paul convinces the commander to allow him to speak to the crowd (Acts 21:32–40).

Paul, speaking in Hebrew, shares his spiritual journey with the crowd. He explains his life before he placed his faith in Christ (Acts 22:1–5), the circumstances that brought him to the Messiah (Acts 22:6–16), and how his life had changed since that day on the road to Damascus (Acts 22:17–21). While he speaks the people quietly listen—until he mentions that God called him to minister to Gentiles. Hearing Paul speak of the despised Gentiles, the crowd erupts in mayhem as people throw cloaks into the air and shout for Paul's death. As a result, the Roman commander, Claudius, moves Paul inside the barracks (Acts 22:22–29).

The next day Claudius assembles the Sanhedrin, composed of Ananias the high priest and his seventy-member Council, in order to judge Paul's guilt or innocence. Paul brilliantly divides the Sanhedrin by positioning his case as a referendum on whether or not God could resurrect a person from the dead—a belief held by those on the Council belonging to the party of the Pharisees but denied by the Sadducees. Instead of rendering a verdict, the members of the Sanhedrin fight among themselves, causing Claudius to move Paul back to the barracks for his own protection (Acts 22:30–23:11).

When Paul's nephew overhears members of the Sanhedrin conspiring to kill the apostle, he reports the plot to the commander. Because of the size of the threat (over forty men have sworn not to eat or drink until they have killed Paul), Claudius decides to move Paul to Caesarea in order for Governor Felix to judge him. Claudius uses the cover of night and the protection of seventy cavalry and two hundred soldiers to deliver Paul there without incident. At Caesarea the governor keeps Paul in custody in his palace, the Praetorium, until Paul's accusers arrive and make their case (Acts 23:12–25). This begins the **first imprisonment** of the three Paul endured over the next several years.

Five days later, Ananias the high priest and some other Jewish leaders arrive in Caesarea with Tertullus, their attorney. The apostle's trial unfolds in an orderly fashion with the prosecutor making his case by first properly addressing the governor and then making three accusations against the accused: Paul stirred up dissention among the Jews around the world, he served as the leader of a sect, and he even tried to desecrate the temple (Acts 24:2–9). When the governor gives Paul permission, the missionary delivers his own defense (Acts 24:10–21). He declares that his accusers cannot prove their charges, and he points out that they could not even prove him guilty at his previous trial just days earlier, which they themselves officiated. He also notes to the governor the conspicuous absence of his original antagonists, the Asian Jews. After listening to both sides of the argument, the governor decides to postpone his judgment until Commander Claudius arrives (Acts 24:22–23).

Whether Claudius ever arrives we don't know. We do know, however, that Felix keeps Paul in custody for two years in order to placate the Jews, though he does allow Paul limited freedom with access to his friends. During his imprisonment Paul communicates how to have faith in Christ to the governor and his wife Drusilla.

At the end of the two years, Porcius Festus succeeds Felix as governor (Acts 24:24–27). Three days after his arrival in Caesarea, Festus travels to Jerusalem where he finds that even after two years the animosity of the Jewish leaders toward Paul has not diminished. They request Festus to send Paul to Jerusalem for his trial, hoping to ambush and kill him somewhere along the sixty-five-mile trip. Instead, Festus invites the influential men to travel to Caesarea for the trial, which occurs about a week and a half later (Acts 25:1–6).

At the trial, Paul's accusers make many serious charges, none of which they can prove. Like Felix before him, however, Festus wants to ingratiate himself with the Jews, so he asks Paul if he would submit to a trial in Jerusalem. Recognizing Festus' offer as a setup, Paul asks that the Roman Emperor hear his case, to which the governor agrees (Acts 25:7–12).

Before leaving for Rome, Festus has Paul present his case before Agrippa—the Jewish king whose great-grandfather tried to kill Jesus in Bethlehem (Matthew 2), whose great-uncle beheaded John the Baptist (Matthew 14) and mocked Jesus (Luke 23), and whose father killed the apostle James with a sword (Acts 12). While making his defense, Paul so powerfully communicates the credibility of the resurrection of Christ that Agrippa exclaims, "In a short time you will persuade me to become a Christian." At the conclusion of the hearing, King Agrippa and Governor Festus recognize Paul's innocence (Acts 25:13–26:32).

Yet Paul's appeal to Caesar persuades them to send Paul to Rome, where he endures his **second imprisonment**. Oddly, Luke devotes more Scripture to the *trip* to Rome (fifty-nine verses) than he does to the *imprisonment* in Rome (sixteen verses). Let's take a look at the adventurous trip.

Festus gives Julius, a centurion of the emperor's special troops—the Augustan cohort—the responsibility for transporting Paul and some other prisoners to Rome. The governor also allows two companions of Paul's to accompany him, Luke and Aristarchus. Using a coastal ship, the party sails in two days from Caesarea to Sidon, one of the two major cities of Phoenicia, or modern-day Lebanon. From Sidon they sail in open waters to Myra, where they board a ship carrying grain from Alexandria, Egypt, to Rome. After a number of days with difficult sailing, they arrive at the harbor of Fair Havens on the southern coast of Crete, five miles from the city of Lasea (Acts 27:1–8).

At Fair Havens the centurion discusses with the ship's pilot and captain whether they should winter there or sail to Phoenix, a more suitable harbor forty miles west. The apostle, having already experienced three shipwrecks, counsels against it. The desire for a better harbor in which to spend the winter motivates the decision makers to take the risk. As soon as a southern wind blows, they set sail (Acts 27:9–13).

Not long after beginning the journey, a violent northeastern wind known as the *Euraquilo* hits the ship with such force that it renders the crew helpless. They can do nothing to control the ship and must allow the wind to drive it wherever it pleases. Two weeks and five hundred miles later, having jettisoned all of the cargo, the 276 passengers find themselves shipwrecked on the island of Malta (Acts 27:14–28:10). After waiting three months for winter to pass, the party travels 330 miles by sea and approximately 140 miles by land to Rome (Acts 28:11–15).

Once in Rome the authorities allow Paul limited freedom. Living in his own rented house, he has several companions during this second imprisonment. In addition to Luke and Aristarchus, he enjoys the company of Timothy (Philippians 1:1; Colossians 1:1), Tychicus, Onesimus, John Mark, Epaphras, Justus, and Demas (Colossians 4:10–14).

Though imprisoned for over two years, the missionary in chains proves quite productive in his work for the Lord Jesus. He teaches Old Testament Scripture and writes four letters, which eventually become part of the New Testament: Ephesians, Philippians, Colossians, and Philemon. He also shares God's love and forgiveness with the various soldiers chained to him (Acts 28:16–31). In his letter to the Christians in Philippi (Philippians 1:12–13), the great apostle writes, "Now I want you to know, brethren, that my circumstances have turned out for the greater progress of the gospel, so that my imprisonment in the cause of Christ has become well known throughout the whole praetorian guard and to everyone else."

PAUL'S WRITINGS DURING THE TRIALS PERIOD

DURING HIS INITIAL ROMAN IMPRISONMENT	BETWEEN HIS ROMAN IMPRISONMENTS	DURING HIS FINAL ROMAN IMPRISONMENT
Ephesians Philippians Colossians Philemon	1 Timothy Titus	2 Timothy

Luke finishes the book of Acts before Paul's case goes before the Roman emperor. From other New Testament books we discover that Rome releases Paul from his second imprisonment. Whether acquitted or declared innocent, Paul's freedom allows him to resume his missionary work before he begins his **third imprisonment**.

Let's trace the apostle's activities just before this final imprisonment. Though we do not possess a definitive itinerary for Paul's travels during this time, Scripture does provide a few clues found in the following chart.

CLUES TO PAUL'S
POSSIBLE ITINERARY BETWEEN HIS ROMAN IMPRISONMENTS

SCRIPTURE	TIMING	COMMENT
"Whenever I go to Spain . . . I will go on by way of you to Spain." (Rom. 15:24, 28)	Written during Paul's third missionary journey	Paul desires to visit the Christians of Rome and to solicit help from them for his missionary trip to Spain.
"My coming to you again . . . as soon as I see how things go with me; and I trust in the Lord that I myself also shall be coming shortly." (Phil. 1:26; 2:23–24)	Written during Paul's initial Roman imprisonment	During Paul's imprisonment, he writes the Philippian Church in Macedonia that he desires to visit them as soon as the authorities release him.

"And at the same time also prepare me a lodging; for I hope that through your prayers I shall be given to you." (Philem. 22)	Written during Paul's initial Roman imprisonment	Paul writes to Philemon in the city of Colossae, saying that he desires to visit Philemon when Rome releases Paul from imprisonment.
"As I urged you upon my departure for Macedonia, remain on at Ephesus." (1 Tim. 1:3)	Written between Paul's Roman imprisonments	Apparently, Paul visits Ephesus, the city in which he ministered for three years, and departs for Macedonia.
"For this reason I left you in Crete." (Titus 1:5)	Written between Paul's Roman imprisonments	Paul and Titus plant churches on the island of Crete between the two Roman imprisonments.
"Make every effort to come to me at Nicopolis, for I have decided to spend the winter there." (Titus 3:12)	Written between Paul's Roman imprisonments	Paul asks Titus to meet him in Nicopolis, located in Greece.
"Bring the cloak which I left at Troas." (2 Tim. 4:13)	Written during Paul's final Roman imprisonment	Paul definitely visits the city of Troas in between his two Roman imprisonments.
"Erastus remained at Corinth, but Trophimus I left sick at Miletus." (2 Tim. 4:20)	Written during Paul's final Roman imprisonment	Paul visits Corinth in Achaia, south of Macedonia, and Miletus, a port thirty-six miles south of Ephesus.

Scholars debate the order of his itinerary, but Paul definitely visits the cities of Ephesus, Miletus, and Troas on the west coast of modern-day Turkey and, possibly, Colossae to see Philemon. He also visits cities in modern-day Greece, specifically Corinth and possibly Philippi and Nicopolis.

Paul also forges new work during this time by planting churches with Titus on the island of Crete. Whether he ever makes it to Spain, we have no certainty. Although Clement, an early respected Church leader who lived at the end of the first century, says that the great missionary reached his objective.

After Emperor Nero burns Rome and blames the arson on the city's Christian population, fierce persecution arises against the followers of Christ. At some point, the Roman authorities arrest Paul again and take him back to Rome. Rather than restricting him to the confinement of a house, this time the officials send him, most likely, to the Mamertine prison with its deplorable conditions, including wearing chains, lacking proper food, going without sanitary facilities, fighting off rats, and breathing stale air.

ROMAN CAESARS REIGNING DURING THE NEW TESTAMENT

CAESAR	DATES	SCRIPTURE
Augustus (Octavian)	27 BC–AD 14	Luke 2:1
Tiberius	AD 14–37	Luke 3:1
Caligula (Gaius)	AD 37–41	
Claudius	AD 41–54	Acts 11:28; 17:7; 18:2
Nero	AD 54–68	Acts 25:11; Philippians 4:22
Galba	AD 68	
Otho	AD 69	
Vitellius	AD 69	
Vespasian	AD 69–79	
Titus	AD 79–81	
Domitian	AD 81–96	

Tradition says that the Romans execute Paul by chopping off his head, a death Paul foreshadows in his last later to Timothy: "For I am already being poured out as a drink offering, and the time of my departure has come" (2 Timothy 4:6). Just as Jews poured out a drink offering in its entirety on the altar as an act of worship before God, Paul offered to God the blood that would flow from his neck after the executioner cut off his head—a final act of worship for the Lord Jesus whom he so deeply loved.

Not only does Paul suffer during the Trials Period of the Church, but others do as well. History also points to Peter suffering a martyr's death in Rome. Because Peter did not possess Roman citizenship, the law did not provide for him a quick and relatively painless death as it did for Paul. Peter has to suffer the cross as His master had suffered it, a fate that Christ had prophesied in John 21:18–19. Additionally, the beloved apostle John, well advanced in years, describes himself in the first chapter of the book of Revelation as a fellow partaker in tribulation as he lives in exile on the island of Patmos.

Though the Church and its greatest heroes suffer terrible persecution during the Trials Period of the Church, an incredible future awaits. In the next chapter we'll learn about the Triumphant Period of the Church from the book of Revelation. There we will catch an inadequate glimpse of the incredibly wonderful future that the followers of Christ will one day experience.

The next section helps us to better grasp the locations of the events surrounding the three imprisonments of the Trials Period of the Church.

WHERE?

Once again as in the Public Period, the events of the Trials Period of the Church occur throughout the Mediterranean region. Let's begin by identifying the locations of the events surrounding the first imprisonment that we find in Acts 21–26. Paul ends his third missionary trip in the city of Jerusalem (1). The Roman commander Claudius Lysias arrests the returning missionary and transports him sixty-five miles to Caesarea (2), the beautiful city built by Herod the Great on the shore of the Mediterranean Sea in honor of Caesar Augustus. There Paul endures his first imprisonment for two years.

Paul's Journey to his First Imprisonment

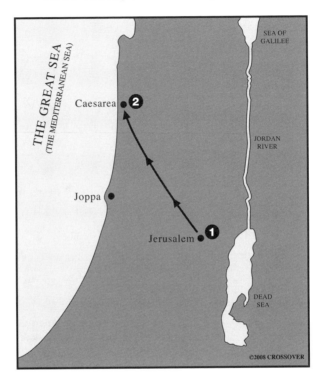

Paul's appeal to have his case tried before the emperor sets up the events for his second imprisonment, which we discover in Acts 27–28. Paul leaves Caesarea (1) and sails in one day to the Phoenician city of Sidon (2), approximately seventy miles to the north. Since the prevailing winds blow from the west, the ship sails on the east side of the island of Cyprus along the coast of Cilicia, landing at Myra (3) in the Roman province of Lycia on the southern coast of modern-day Turkey. At Myra the centurion finds a grain ship (Acts 27:6) on which his soldiers and prisoners could continue their sea voyage. They sail the next 130 miles with great difficulty, taking many days to reach Cnidus (4), situated on the southwest tip of Asia Minor. Because of the unfavorable winds, the ship sails to the east and south of the island of Crete, making port at Fair

Havens (5). Attempting to sail another forty miles in order to spend the winter in the Cretan harbor of Phoenix, the ship tosses for two weeks in a violent storm that carries them between five and six hundred miles off course to the eighteen-mile-long, eight-mile-wide island of Malta (6).

Paul's Journey to his Second Imprisonment

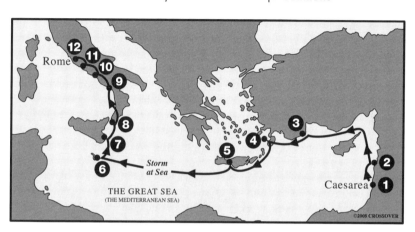

After spending the winter on the island of Malta, the centurion loads Paul and the other prisoners onto another boat. They sail north eighty miles to Syracuse (7), the capital of the island of Sicily; then seventy miles to Rhegium (8), located on the "toe" of Italy; and then, finishing the sea portion of the trip, 180 miles in only two days to Puteoli (9), the port of Naples. To complete their trip, they travel by land another 150 miles north on the Appian Way, the famous Roman road. As the party makes its way to the imperial capital, believers travel forty-three miles from Rome to intercept Paul at the Market of Appius (10). Other believers from Rome meet the apostle at Three Inns (11), located ten miles closer to the capital. After several months and hundreds of miles, the faithful missionary arrives in Rome (12).

After Paul's release from his initial Roman imprisonment, he travels to various places. Though we do not know the exact itinerary, we know that he visits the cities of Miletus (1), Ephesus (2), and Troas (3) in the Roman province of Asia and, possibly, Colossae (4). He also visits Corinth (5) in the Roman province of Achaia as well as Nicopolis (6) and, possibly, Philippi (7) in the Roman province of Macedonia. We know he plants churches with Titus on the island of Crete (8), but we do not know if he ever makes it to Spain (9). When the Romans take Paul back to Rome (10) for his third imprisonment, they most likely put him in the Mamertine prison before executing him. According to tradition, Paul's demise takes place on the Roman road known as the Ostian Way, memorialized today in Rome by the Church of St. Paul of Three Fountains.

Paul's Journey to his Third Imprisonment

Now let's determine when each of Paul's imprisonments occur.

WHEN?

Scripture provides several excellent pieces of evidence that help us determine quite confidently the time frame of Paul's first two imprisonments. For locating the dates for Paul's third imprisonment (his second

Roman imprisonment), we must refer to historical events recorded outside of the Bible.

From the previous chapter we know that Paul finishes his third missionary journey around the Pentecost that occurred during the month of May in AD 57. Luke provides clear time markers in Acts 21–25 for both the events leading up to Paul's first imprisonment as well as the length of Paul's incarceration in the Caesarea prison.

Luke diligently chronicles the daily events at the beginning and end of Paul's imprisonment. In Acts 24:27 Luke summarizes the vast majority of Paul's time in Caesarea in five words: "After two years had passed." Some researchers account for this broad brush by suggesting Luke may have used this time to travel to Palestine in order to research the material needed to write his Gospel on the life of Christ.

From Luke's extensive time markers, we discover that no more than a couple of weeks pass between Paul's arrival in Jerusalem and his imprisonment in Caesarea. Once imprisoned, however, the apostle is held two entire years, from approximately June AD 57 to somewhere between August and September AD 59. The reason we specify between August and September will become clear in a moment.

SCRIPTURAL TIME MARKERS
PRECEDING AND INCLUDING THE FIRST IMPRISONMENT

Acts 21:27	"Seeing him in the temple"
Acts 24:11	"No more than twelve days ago I went up to Jerusalem to worship" (in the temple)
Acts 24:27	"After two years had passed"

Now let's determine (1) the time that elapses while the centurion transports Paul to Rome for his second imprisonment and (2) the length of time Paul spends in chains in the imperial city during his initial Roman imprisonment. Again Luke provides a detailed time log for us to follow in Acts 27–28.

We can observe three primary time markers in the chart below. First, Luke writes in Acts 27:9 how dangerous sailing from Fair Havens has become, noting the completion of "the fast." The fast refers to the Feast of the Atonement that occurs in October AD 59. Sailing across the Mediterranean Sea in those days ceased on November 11 due to the dangerous weather conditions. Because of this verse we have a fairly accurate idea of when this part of the voyage occurs. We don't know exactly, but based on the number of days it takes to reach Fair Havens and the amount of time Luke indicates they stay there, it appears that the group probably leaves late summer or early autumn of AD 59, sometime around August and September.

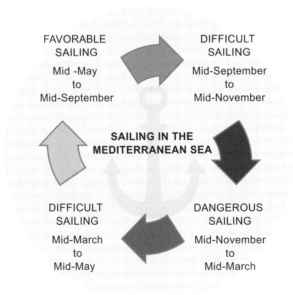

FAVORABLE SAILING
Mid -May to Mid-September

DIFFICULT SAILING
Mid-September to Mid-November

SAILING IN THE MEDITERRANEAN SEA

DIFFICULT SAILING
Mid-March to Mid-May

DANGEROUS SAILING
Mid-November to Mid-March

We derive our second primary time marker from Acts 28:11, where Luke records that the party stays on the island of Malta for three months, which probably represents all of November and December AD 59 and

PUTTING TOGETHER THE PUZZLE OF THE NEW TESTAMENT

January AD 60. This puts them setting sail again probably in mid-February of AD 60, which we know marks the earliest that first-century sailors would dare begin sailing for fear of winter storms. After leaving the island of Malta, it takes only a couple of weeks to reach Rome, allowing them to arrive around the beginning of March at the earliest.

The third primary time marker covers the amount of time Paul remains in his initial Roman imprisonment. Luke writes in Acts 28:30 that Paul stays chained to a Roman soldier for two full years in his rented house. This clue means that the Roman authorities do not release Paul before spring AD 62.

SCRIPTURAL TIME MARKERS
PRECEDING AND INCLUDING THE SECOND IMPRISONMENT

Acts 27:9	"The voyage was now dangerous, since even the fast was already over"
Acts 28:11	"At the end of three months"
Acts 28:30	"He stayed two full years"

To identify the amount of time covered by the events leading to and including Paul's third and final imprisonment, we must consult not only Scripture but other resources as well. Long-standing church tradition states that both Peter and Paul die in Rome as martyrs under Nero in AD 67. Certainly, we can set the latest date of Paul's execution at June AD 68, because Nero himself dies on June 9, AD 68.

So if Paul gains his liberty from his second imprisonment as early as spring of AD 62, then he has approximately five years to spread the message of God's love and forgiveness to the nations, possibly making it to Spain. Halfway through Paul's window of freedom, Nero burns the city of Rome. Blaming the arson on Christians intensifies persecution throughout the empire. Arrested in AD 67, for what reason we do not know, Paul is sent to Rome. Later that year, Nero has Paul beheaded.

HISTORICAL TIME MARKERS
PRECEDING AND INCLUDING THE THIRD IMPRISONMENT

Spring AD 62	Earliest release date for Paul from second imprisonment
July 19, AD 64	Nero burns the city of Rome
Summer AD 64	Nero blames Christians for the fire, and persecution begins
AD 67	Paul imprisoned for the third time (second time in Rome)
AD 67	Nero executes Paul
June 9, AD 68	Nero dies

We now have identified a little over two years devoted to the events preceding and including Paul's Caesarean imprisonment, almost three years spent in travel and incarceration for the second imprisonment, and finally about five years when Paul did mission work and endured his third imprisonment, which ended in his death. Adding these three time segments together gives us the total time covered during the Trials Period of the Church: from May AD 57 to sometime in AD 67, or approximately **ten years**. The following chart summarizes the three imprisonments of the apostle Paul, whose missionary activity dominates the scriptural information passed down to us about the Church's Trials Period.

TIMETABLE FOR THE TRIALS PERIOD OF THE CHURCH

IMPRISONMENT	DATE	SCRIPTURE
Preceding Events (In Jerusalem)	Occur over a two-week period during May AD 57	Acts 21:17–23:22
First Imprisonment (In Caesarea)	≈ June AD 57 to ≈ August/September AD 59	Acts 23:23–26:32
Preceding Events (Voyage to Rome)	≈ August/September AD 59 to ≈ February AD 60	Acts 27:1–28:15
Second Imprisonment (1st in Rome)	≈ February AD 60 to ≈ Spring AD 62	Acts 28:16–28:31
Preceding Events (Further mission work)	≈ Spring AD 62 to AD 67	1 Timothy 1:3; Titus 1:5; 3:12; 2 Timothy 4:13, 20
Third Imprisonment (2nd in Rome)	AD 67	2 Timothy 1:8, 16; 2:9; 4:16

Let's now turn our attention once again to the theme of the Bible and consider God's purpose behind all that occurs during the Trial Period of the Church.

WHY?

Peter and Philip's emphasis on the central theme of the Bible during the previous New Testament time period, the Public Period of the Church, does not surprise us: The Lord Jesus had recently risen from the dead, commissioning His followers to diligently spread the message of God's love and forgiveness. Nor do Paul's great missionary efforts seem inappropriate in light of Christ's dramatic appearance to him on the road to Damascus, appointing him to take the gospel to the Gentiles. Yet what about the Trials Period of the Church, when persecution placed believers on defense and the Church's great leaders spent years at a time in prison, sometimes suffering inhumane public deaths? Do we find an emphasis on **God receiving glory by restoring fellowship between the nations and Himself through His Son, Jesus Christ?** Most definitely!

Consider the following sampling of verses associated with each of the three imprisonments. You will find some phrases italicized for emphasis so that you will clearly see that Paul never loses sight of God's heart for the nations.

- **First Imprisonment (In Caesarea):** "And the Lord said, . . . '*the Gentiles, to whom I am sending you*, to open their eyes so that they may turn from darkness to light and from the dominion of Satan to God, in order that they may receive forgiveness of sins and an inheritance among those who have been sanctified by faith in Me.' Consequently, King Agrippa, I did not prove disobedient to the heavenly vision, but *kept declaring . . . and even to the Gentiles, that they should repent and turn to God*" (Acts 26:15–20).

- **Second Imprisonment (Initial Roman imprisonment):** "Let it be known to you therefore, that *this salvation of God has been sent to the Gentiles*; they will also listen" (Acts 28:28); "To be specific, that the Gentiles are fellow heirs and fellow members of the body, and fellow partakers of the promise in Christ Jesus through the gospel, of which I was made a minister, according to the gift of God's grace which was given to me according to the working of His power. To me, the very least of all saints, this grace was given, *to preach to the Gentiles the unfathomable riches of Christ*" (Ephesians 3:6–8); "Now I want you to know, brethren, that *my circumstances have turned out for the greater progress of the gospel, so that my imprisonment in the cause of Christ has become well known throughout the whole praetorian guard and to everyone else*" (Philippians 1:12–13); "To whom

God willed to make known what is the riches of the glory of this mystery among the Gentiles, which is Christ in you, the hope of glory. And *we proclaim Him, admonishing every man and teaching every man with all wisdom, that we may present every man complete in Christ*. And for this purpose also I labor, striving according to His power, which mightily works within me" (Colossians 1:27–29).

- **Between Roman Imprisonments:** "It is a trustworthy statement, deserving full acceptance, that *Christ Jesus came into the world to save sinners*, among whom I am foremost of all" (1 Timothy 1:15); "For *the grace of God has appeared, bringing salvation to all men*" (Titus 2:11).

- **Third Imprisonment (Final Roman imprisonment):** "But the Lord stood with me, and strengthened me, *in order that through me the proclamation might be fully accomplished, and that all the Gentiles might hear*" (2 Timothy 4:17).

So even in prison, Paul's heart beats for the nations. Even during the last days of his life, when a less-committed follower of Christ might tend to focus fearfully on impending death, the great apostle could not cease thinking about the tremendous need for all people to have the opportunity to hear, understand, and accept the message of the long-awaited Messiah, the risen Lord Jesus Christ.

Let's turn our attention now to another apostle who suffers martyrdom during the Trials Period of the Church, James, the half-brother of Jesus.

WHO?

We've looked in the previous chapters at the four Gospel writers (Matthew, Mark, Luke, and John) and the two pillars of the Church (Peter and Paul). We now come to two half-brothers of Jesus, James and Jude, as we continue learning about the eight contributors to the New Testament. The two half-brothers both wrote epistles that God providentially places in the Bible. Let's consider James here and Jude in the next chapter.

What can we learn about James, the half brother of Jesus? Scripture devotes several verses to James as well as several verses to the half-brothers of Jesus as a group. From these two groups of references, we learn the following about James—making certain, however, that we don't confuse this James with the other men named James in the Bible, such as James the brother of John, or James the son of Alphaeus, or James the father of Judas (not Iscariot).

Matthew 13:55, Mark 6:3, and Jude 1:1 identify the names of Jesus' half-brothers: James, Joseph, Simon, and Judas (who is later called Jude). Another verse (1 Corinthians 9:5) implies that James may have had a wife. John 7:3–5 and Acts 1:14 indicate that the Lord's half-brothers do not believe in Him as the Messiah until after the resurrection. Yet later, in his epistle, James describes himself as a bond servant of the Lord Jesus Christ (James 1:1). This change of heart could have occurred between Jesus' resurrection and ascension when the risen Lord appears to James (1 Corinthians 15:7), thus qualifying him to serve as an apostle (Galatians 1:19).

In Acts 1:14 we find James in the upper room waiting on the promise of the Holy Spirit. By Acts 12:17 James has become the primary leader of the church in Jerusalem, and everyone recognizes him as such (Acts 15:13–20; 21:18; Galatians 2:9, 12).

The rest of what we know about James comes from tradition. Both Josephus, the non-Christian historian from the first century, and Eusebius, quoting a second-century Christian historian, write about Jewish priests in Jerusalem martyring James. The later source perhaps embellishes the account, suggesting that the priests push James off the pinnacle of the temple; and when the fall does not kill him, the crowd stones James, finishing him off by hitting him with a club. Most historians believe the martyrdom of James occurs around AD 61 or AD 62, just a few years before the martyrdom of Peter and Paul.

THE WRITINGS OF JAMES

James

Whereas Paul focuses on faith, James in his writing focuses on works—so much so that his emphasis has confused many devoted Christians. For example, note the italicized phrases in the verses that follow. Paul writes in Romans 3:28, "For we maintain that a man is *justified by faith* apart from works of the Law." Yet in James 2:24, the Lord's half-brother writes, "You see that a man is *justified by works*, and not by faith alone." How do we reconcile these two authors of inerrant Scripture?

We must consider the main point each author desires to make. Paul, in his vigilance against the Judaizers adding anything to the gospel of grace, declares that people receive a right relationship with God through faith alone in the Lord Jesus Christ. Paul focuses on how non-Christians appropriate righteousness. James, on the other hand, focuses on how Christians demonstrate the righteousness that they receive. James declares that if a person truly has a right relationship with God, then he or she will diligently seek to live a life that honors God. Paul deals with the *reason* (faith in Christ) for salvation; and James deals with the *result* (good works) of salvation.

PAUL	Justified by faith	Appropriation of righteousness	Reason for salvation
JAMES	Justified by works	Demonstration of righteousness	Result of salvation

So Paul and James do not disagree with each other. Their statements about justification (a right relationship with God) simply stress different aspects of the subject. One writer emphasizes how to *appropriate* righteousness, and the other emphasized how to *demonstrate* righteousness. Further, we can look at other verses to discover that each author actually supports the emphasis of the other.

	REASON FOR SALVATION	RESULT OF SALVATION
PAUL	The gift of God (Ephesians 2:8–9)	Works (Ephesians 2:10)
JAMES	The exercise of His will (James 1:18)	Works (James 2:17)

James agrees with Paul—works do not make us right with God—when he writes in James 1:18 and 21, "In the exercise of His will He brought us forth by the word of truth, so that we might be, as it were, the first fruits among His creatures. . . . In humility receive the word implanted, which is able to save your souls." Paul agrees with James—works provide the evidence of genuine salvation—when he pens in Ephesians 2:10, "For we are His workmanship, created in Christ Jesus for good works, which God prepared beforehand, that we should walk in them."

FOR NEXT TIME

If you are having an extremely busy week:	If you have a little extra time:	If you can't get enough:
read Jude.	add Revelation 1–5, 19–22.	add Revelation 6–18.

PERIOD #8

PERIOD #8

The Church's Triumphant Period

As we learned in the previous chapter, the Church's Trials Period ended much the same way as Christ's Trials Period—in despair and gloom. We found from the book of 2 Timothy that the great apostle Paul waited in a Roman prison for his execution, or as Paul described it, to have his life poured out as a drink offering. From history we know that the Roman government not only beheaded the greatest missionary of all time but also crucified the apostle Peter about the same time. With these two apostolic pillars eliminated, the Church's future appeared quite dark and dismal.

Fortunately, the writers of Scripture added one more period of New Testament history. Just as the Gospels powerfully describe the resurrection from the grave of the Lord Jesus Christ, the last book of the Bible paints a glorious future for the Church. In this last historical period of the New Testament, we discover the ultimate destiny of the Church as God consummates all of history around the throne of heaven.

Before we gaze into the Church's triumphant future, we need to once again assemble our puzzle. Take a moment to complete the following chart by identifying the two historical eras of the New Testament and the four periods associated with each era.

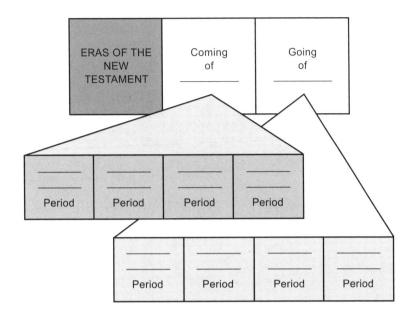

As you complete the next chart by naming the key items for each of the above historical periods, try to reflect on what you've learned about each item. If you forget a particular key item, try to finish as much of the chart as possible before referring to previous chapters for the answers.

CHRIST'S _____ PERIOD: 7 GROUPS	CHRIST'S _____ PERIOD: 7 THEMES	CHRIST'S _____ PERIOD: 7 DAYS
Born to _____ and _____	Inspires the _____	_____ occurs on Sunday
Worshiped by _____	Instructs the _____	_____ occurs on Monday
Honored by _____ and _____	Infuriates the _____	_____ occurs on Tuesday
Sought by _____ and _____	Causes _____	_____ occurs on Wednesday
Taught by temple _____	Cures the _____	_____ and _____ occur on Thursday
Baptized by _____	Casts out _____	_____ occurs on Friday
Tempted by _____	Reveals that we can be _____	_____ occurs on Saturday

CHRIST'S _____ PERIOD: 3 CONFIDENCE BUILDERS	CHURCH'S _____ PERIOD: 3 EVENTS	CHURCH'S _____ PERIOD: 3 ADVANCES
_____	_____	By _____ to the _____
_____	_____	By _____ to the _____
_____	_____	By _____ to the _____

CHURCH'S _____ PERIOD: 3 IMPRISONMENTS
Paul imprisoned in _____
Paul imprisoned in _____
Paul imprisoned in _____

Let's turn our attention now to the final historical period of the New Testament. What happens to the Church?

WHAT?

The Trials Period of the Church brings an end to past biblical history. The Triumphant Period of the Church, on the other hand, will occur in the future. The parenthesis of time existing between the Trials and Triumphant Periods includes the days in which we currently live. Presently, the gospel continues to advance to the ends of the earth.

PAST	(PRESENT)	FUTURE
Trials Period of the Church	(The days in which we currently live)	Triumphant Period of the Church

We know a lot about the events that will occur in the future Triumphant Period because of prophecies found throughout both the Old and the New Testaments. The vast majority of predictions about the Triumphant Period from the New Testament come from prophecies the apostle John records in the book of Revelation.

THE CHURCH'S TRIUMPHANT PERIOD

The Book of Revelation

John divides his book into three main sections: the things that he had seen, the things that are, and the things that shall take place after these things (Revelation 1:19). Chapter one deals with the things that John had seen by describing his vision of Christ in heaven. In chapters two and three John writes about the things contemporary to his own day and time. These things include short messages to seven different churches in Asia (the western portion of modern-day Turkey) concerning their spiritual condition. The third section of his book, "the things which shall take place after these things" (Revelation 1:19; 4:1), covers chapters four through twenty-two. In these pages of Scripture John foretells the future of the Church. This apocalypse, or revelation, will climax in **the presentation of the Church** before the throne of heaven as the people redeemed by the blood of the Messiah worship the Lord Jesus Christ for all eternity. As we delve into the Triumphant Period, we will focus on the third section of the book of Revelation in order to understand the future of the Church.

OUTLINE OF REVELATION
(REVELATION 1:19)

PAST	PRESENT	FUTURE
The things which John had seen	The things which are	The things which shall take place after these things
Revelation 1	Revelation 2–3	Revelation 4–22

Not all Bible scholars teach, however, that the events of Revelation 4–22 occur in the future. Four main approaches to interpreting the book's content exist. The Preterists see all the events in the book as having already historically occurred by the time Jerusalem fell to the Romans in AD 70. The Historicists, who have an interpretive approach similar to the Preterists, believe that the book depicts historical events occurring from biblical times to the present. The Idealists interpret Revelation as being neither historical nor prophetic, but symbolic of the ongoing struggle between good and evil. The Futurists maintain that chapters four through twenty-two describe events that have yet to take place. We will follow the Futurist approach.

Let's look at how the future of the Church unfolds throughout this third section of John's Revelation.

HOW?

The contents of Revelation 4–22 can initially appear confusing, yet on closer inspection we find that the chapters detail several distinct prophetic events that await the Church during the Triumphant Period. Let's identify each.

The first prophecy that deals with the future covers fifteen chapters (Revelation 4–18). The apostle John and the Lord Jesus Christ calls this event **the great tribulation** (Revelation 7:14; Matthew 24:21) because of the tremendous suffering and affliction that will occur.

John depicts the great tribulation in a series of three pronouncements, each consisting of seven judgments. The three pronouncements involve seven seals in a book, seven trumpets, and seven bowls. Each of the judgments brings with it a catastrophic result on the earth, as the chart below demonstrates. The striking similarity of the last judgment in each pronouncement causes scholars to disagree on whether the three pronouncements occur concurrently or consecutively. Either way, the great tribulation will certainly involve tremendous suffering.

THE JUDGMENTS OF THE GREAT TRIBULATION

3 PRONOUNCEMENTS	SEALS (Revelation 6:1–8:5)	TRUMPETS (Revelation 8:6–15:8)	BOWLS (Revelation 16:1–18:24)
7 JUDGMENTS EACH	Conquering	One-third of earth burned	Sores
	Slaying	One-third of sea destroyed	All sea life dies
	Famine	One-third of water poisoned	Water becomes blood
	Killing	One-third of sky darkened	Scorching heat
	Martyrdom	Locusts for five months	Darkness
	Great earthquake	One-third of mankind killed	Gathering for battle of Armageddon
	Thunder, lightning, earthquake	Thunder, earthquake, hail	Thunder, lightning, earthquake, hail

We find John's next prophecy in Revelation 19:1–16. These verses, especially verses 11–16, depict **the second coming of Christ**. Remember what the angels told the disciples on the Mount of Olives as the followers of Christ gazed into the clouds after the Messiah ascended into heaven? "This Jesus, who has been taken up from you into heaven, will come in just the same way as you have watched Him go into heaven" (Acts 1:11). The event depicted in this portion of John's revelation refers to their announcement. The angels do not stand alone in predicting Christ's glorious return. Others, including the Old Testament prophet Zechariah (Zechariah 14:4) and even the Lord Jesus himself (Luke 21:27), referenced a return of the Messiah.

John's description of Jesus in His second coming forms a stark contrast to Jesus' first appearance. Rather than the suffering servant riding a peaceful donkey, the King of Kings mounts a white horse of war; rather than a crown of thorns sitting on His head, the Lord of Lords wears many diadems; rather than Jesus alone because His disciples deserted Him, the armies of heaven follow behind Him. The most striking contrast, however, deals with Christ's mission. During His first appearance Jesus came to reconcile the nations to God by dying on the cross in order to pay the penalty for mankind's disobedience. Christ's second appearance stresses not mercy and grace but judgment as He pours out the fierce wrath of God on those in every nation who do not possess a right relationship with God. We discover in the next prophecy how Christ will execute His judgment.

In his third prophecy, found in Revelation 19:17–20:3, John announces **the defeat of three enemies** of God at the second coming of Christ. During the great tribulation, a wicked triad rises to power, uniting the nations of the earth against God and His people. The first of these three enemies appears in Revelation 12, with verse 9 giving a thorough description of him: "And the great dragon was thrown down, the serpent of old who is called the devil and Satan, who deceives the whole world; he was thrown down to the earth, and his angels were thrown down with him."

The other two members of this evil trio appear in Revelation 13. The first half of the chapter (vv. 1–10) speaks of a beast coming up out of the sea. Many refer to this beast as the Antichrist. Here John paints the picture of a worldwide political leader being given his power, throne, and authority by the dragon. Everyone who dwells on the earth worships this beast, except those whose names have been written from the foundation of the world in the book of life. Against these saints this beast wages war.

In the second half of chapter thirteen, John details another beast coming up out of the earth. This enemy serves as a religious leader who uses great signs to persuade those who dwell on the earth to worship the first beast, the Antichrist. This second beast puts to death the people who refuse to worship the Antichrist. Additionally, the beast out of the earth—later called the false prophet in Revelation 19:20—makes everyone receive a mark on either the right hand or forehead in order to buy or sell. John says the mark of the beast calculates to the number six hundred and sixty-six, or simply 666.

At the second coming of Christ, the three vile enemies assemble together with the kings of the earth and their armies in order to wage war against the King of Kings and His heavenly army (Revelation 19:19). Many refer to this great battle as the battle of Armageddon. Based on John's prophecy, it is not much of a fight. First, one of the heavenly hosts throws both the Antichrist and the false prophet into the lake of fire, which burns with brimstone (Revelation 19:20). Next, the Lord effortlessly kills the rest by simply speaking (Revelation 19:21). Finally, an angel captures the dragon, the serpent of old, binds him with a chain, and throws him into the abyss where the devil stays for a thousand years (Revelation 20:1–3).

THREE ENEMIES OF GOD

NAME	INTRODUCTION	DEFEAT
The dragon, the serpent of old, the devil, Satan	Revelation 12:9	Revelation 20:1–3
The beast out of the sea (often referred to as the Antichrist)	Revelation 13:1–10	Revelation 19:20
The beast out of the earth, the false prophet	Revelation 13:11–18	Revelation 19:20

John writes about the next prophetic event in Revelation 20:4–10, which involves a thousand years of peace on earth as Christ and His followers reign (Revelation 20:6). At the beginning of this thousand-year reign of peace, which many refer to as **the millennium**, God resurrects the believers who died during the great tribulation (Revelation 20:5). At the end of the millennium, God releases Satan, who deceives the nations into launching one final attack on the saints (Revelation 20:7–8). As Satan's army gathers on a broad plain surrounding the beloved city of Jerusalem, God devours the rebellious army with fire from heaven (Revelation 20:9) and throws the devil into the lake of fire and brimstone, where he along with the beast and the false prophet experience torment forever and ever (Revelation 20:10).

In the last five verses of Revelation 20, John moves to the prophetic event that follows the millennium. Here the apostle presents the solemn scene of Christ sitting on a **great white throne of judgment**. Before Christ stand all the wicked who have ever lived. First, the Lord uses a number of books—which record the deeds of the wicked—to judge them (Revelation 20:12–13). Then, the Lord reviews the book of life to find any of the names of the wicked (Revelation 20:15). He finds none of their names because they never trusted Him to make them right with

God; so He throws all of them into the lake of fire where Satan, the Antichrist, and the false prophet already reside in torment.

John records one final prophecy in the last two chapters of Revelation. In Revelation 21 and 22, John describes heaven and earth passing away as God replaces them with **a new heaven and a new earth** (Revelation 21:1–2). In the remaining verses John emphasizes the blessedness of redeemed people living with God for the rest of eternity (Revelation 21:3–8) and the glory of the New Jerusalem (Revelation 21:9–22:5). What a mighty climax to the Triumphant Period of the Church!

Though we find the vast majority of our information about the Triumphant Period of the Church in the book of Revelation, other New Testament books also contain prophecies about the future events of the Church. Interestingly, John does not mention one particularly famous prophetic event in his revelation. Most people refer to this prophecy as **the rapture of the Church**.

The apostle Paul provides the most information about the rapture in 1 Thessalonians 4:13–18. Here we find Jesus Christ descending from heaven but not all the way to earth. With Him come the Christians who have previously died, or as the Scripture says, who have fallen asleep (1 Thessalonians 4:14). While Christ waits in the air, the dead Christians immediately followed by the living Christians rise to meet Him (1 Thessalonians 4:16–17). Now you may wonder how dead Christians can both descend with Christ and rise to meet Him. To comprehend this marvelous affair, you must understand that when believers die, their spirits instantly go to live with the Lord. They do not receive their new, resurrected bodies that the Scripture promises (see 1 Corinthians 15:35–58; Philippians 3:21) until the rapture. At that moment all Christians—those dead in Christ and those still alive on the earth—will receive resurrected bodies and live physically with the Lord.

Taken together these **seven prophecies** summarize the future events that will one day occur during the Triumphant Period of the Church.

For now we will put the rapture of the Church at the beginning of the list. We provide the rationale for the order of these prophecies under the When? section.

SEVEN PROPHECIES OF THE CHURCH'S TRIUMPHANT PERIOD

The rapture of the Church	1 Thessalonians 4:13–18
The great tribulation	Revelation 4–18
The second coming of Christ	Revelation 19:1–16
The defeat of three enemies	Revelation 19:17–20:3
The millennium	Revelation 20:4–10
The great white throne of judgment	Revelation 20:11–15
The new heaven and new earth	Revelation 21–22

Let's look now at the general locations where each of these prophecies will be fulfilled.

WHERE?

In the previous New Testament historical periods, the events occurred in specific and identifiable geographical locations on earth. The seven prophecies summarizing the future events of the Triumphant Period of the Church, however, have a cosmic range in locations, spanning heaven and earth.

The fulfillment of the seven prophecies of the Triumphant Period of the Church begins in heaven. In 1 Thessalonians 4:16 we read that the Lord Himself will descend from heaven but not come all the way to earth. While the Lord Jesus remains suspended in the air, both deceased and living Christians will be "caught up" to meet Him (1 Thessalonians 4:17). After this incredible experience, Christians remain forever and always with the Lord. Because verse 16 talks about Christians rendezvousing in the clouds, we will make the clouds the location of this prophecy.

Consider the location of the suffering during the great tribulation. Focusing just on the seven trumpets, we find each judgment referencing the entire earth. One-third of the earth burns after the first trumpet blows. One-third of the sea turns to blood after the second trumpet sounds. One-third of all the earth's water becomes poisoned as a result of the judgment announced by the third trumpet. One-third of the sky darkens after the fourth trumpet. All the earth seems affected by the locusts streaming forth after the fifth trumpeting. The sixth trumpet results in one-third of all mankind dying. Though Scripture does not specify the global extent of the lightning and thunder, earthquake, and hail of the seventh trumpet, the overall thrust of the judgments announced by the trumpets affects the entire world.

Scripture provides the exact location for the second coming of Christ, but we must look in the Old Testament for where it will happen. Zechariah, prophesying about the return of Christ (Zechariah 14:1–4), declares,

> Behold, a day is coming for the Lord when the spoil taken from you will be divided among you. For I will gather all the nations against Jerusalem to battle, and the city will be captured, the houses plundered, the women ravished, and half of the city exiled, but the rest of the people will not be cut off from the city. Then the Lord will go forth and fight against those nations, as when He fights on a day of battle. And in that day His feet will stand on the Mount of Olives, which is in front of Jerusalem on the east.

It appears from the prophet Zechariah that the Mount of Olives in Jerusalem becomes a key location during the second coming of Christ as

He wages war against the three enemies and the armies of the earth they have mobilized.

After defeating the three enemies, the Lord (or possibly an angel) throws the beast (the Antichrist) and the false prophet into the lake of fire, which burns with brimstone (Revelation 19:20). The King of Kings has an angel throw the devil in a different place, the abyss. What differentiates the lake of fire from the abyss? The abyss represents a bottomless pit (Revelation 9:1–2), which the Lord controls (Revelation 20:1) and in which He keeps captive many demonic spirits (see Luke 8:30–31; Revelation 11:7; 20:2–3). God prepared the lake of fire, however, not as a place of captivity, but as a place of punishment primarily for the devil and his demonic angels (Matthew 25:41). Many people, even Christians, influenced by cartoons of a red-dressed devil with horns and long, pointed tail, holding a pitchfork, think that Satan rules the lake of fire. Not at all! Far from ruling in hell, the devil will join the beast and the false prophet in the fiery lake of hell at the end of the millennium. There the three notorious enemies of Christ will suffer torment day and night forever (Revelation 20:10).

The three enemies of Christ will spend eternity in the fires of hell, and hell ultimately becomes the permanent dwelling place for all who refuse to embrace Christ and His offer of forgiveness. Currently, all the dead who never received Christ dwell in a place the Old Testament calls *Sheol* and the New Testament identifies as *Hades* (Revelation 20:13). After the white throne of judgment, Christ will send all these non-Christians into the lake of fire (Revelation 20:15).

The location of the millennium is on earth where the Lord and His followers will reign in peace for a thousand years. The location of the great white throne of judgment, however, seems a bit mysterious, because the apostle John in Revelation 20:11 says, "And I saw a great white throne and Him who sat upon it, from whose presence earth and heaven fled away." Based on these verses it appears that between the destruction of the current heaven and earth and the coming of the new heaven and earth, the Lord exercises judgment at the great white throne. If so, then we have no idea where this judgment will occur.

THE SEVEN PROPHECIES OF THE CHURCH'S TRIUMPHANT PERIOD

PROPHECY	LOCATION
The rapture of the Church	In the clouds
The great tribulation	Earth
The second coming of Christ	The Mount of Olives in Jerusalem
The defeat of three enemies	The lake of fire and the abyss
The millennium	Earth
The great white throne of judgment	Not in the old or the new heaven and earth
The new heaven and new earth	The new heaven and new earth

The last prophecy occurs in the new heaven and new earth, with an emphasis on the new city of Jerusalem. Because most of the time (the rest of eternity) of the Triumphant Period takes place in the **new heaven and new earth**, we will make them the main location of the Triumphant Period of the Church.

Having identified where the seven prophecies will occur, let's determine when during the Triumphant Period of the Church they will occur.

WHEN?

Both Paul and Peter (1 Thessalonians 5:2; 2 Peter 3:10), quoting the Lord Jesus (Matthew 24:42–44), compare the timing of the end times to a thief breaking into a house. Just as a homeowner has no inkling when a thief might try to rob his house, neither do we have any idea when God will begin to fulfill the first of these seven prophecies. So we start with the nebulous statement that sometime in the future the rapture will occur, marking the beginning of the Triumphant Period of the Church. However, we do have information on how long the rapture will take. Paul in 1 Corinthians 15:51–52 says, "Behold, I tell you a mystery; we shall not all sleep, but we shall all be changed, in a moment, in a twinkling of an eye, at the last trumpet; for the trumpet will sound, and the dead will be raised imperishable, and we shall be changed." By comparing this passage with 1 Thessalonians 4:13–18 concerning the rapture of the Church, we can surmise that the duration of the rapture will not last long, perhaps the time it takes to blink our eyes.

Disagreement exists regarding the timing of the rapture of the Church in relation to the great tribulation. Many suggest the rapture happens before the great tribulation. Others think God raptures the Church halfway through the tribulation. Still others believe it takes place at the end of the terrible time of suffering and affliction. Perhaps we should pray God raptures us before the tribulation but prepare ourselves to live through the turmoil just in case He doesn't.

THREE VIEWS ON THE RAPTURE OF THE CHURCH

Pre-tribulation	God takes the Church out of the world at the beginning of the great tribulation.
Mid-tribulation	God takes the Church out of the world in the middle of the great tribulation.
Post-tribulation	God takes the Church out of the world at the end of the great tribulation.

As to the duration of the great tribulation, many suggest that this time of suffering lasts seven years. Two main reasons exist for this time frame. Many reason that Revelation 11:2–3 points to the first and second halves of the great tribulation, each lasting three and a half years. Others use Daniel 9:24–27 to buttress their argument. They believe each week in this passage equals a seven-year period of time, as in Leviticus 25:8. So seven weeks plus the sixty-two weeks in verse 25 represent the 483 years (360-day years, not 365-day years) between the issuing of the decree to rebuild Jerusalem (which occurred in 444 BC under King Artaxerxes of Persia) and the coming of the Messiah (which occurred in AD 30). Likewise, the last week of seven years mentioned in Daniel 9:27 refers to the number of years of tribulation found in the book of Revelation, because the last week of years occurs after the Messiah has been cut off (Daniel 9:26), and in the middle of that week of years a time of great desolation and destruction takes place (Daniel 9:27). Others include Daniel 12:11 and Revelation 12:6 to justify the seven-year position.

Neither the second coming of Christ nor the defeat of the three diabolical enemies seems to take long at all. Indeed, Revelation 19:21 shows the defeat of the nations through the Lord's spoken word.

One might think that identifying the duration of the millennium is an easy task. Yet many Bible-believing Christians, known as postmillennialists and a-millennialists, interpret the millennium as either historical or symbolic, respectively. Pre-millennialists see the millennium as prophetic and literal. Fortunately, these groups agree on the most important issues of Scripture, such as salvation through faith in Christ, and they agree to disagree on issues such as the millennium.

THREE VIEWS ON THE MILLENNIUM

Pre-millennial	Believes Christ returns physically to earth at His second coming, where He reigns for a literal 1,000 years
Post-millennial	Believes the 1,000-year reign represents the Church currently spreading the message of God's forgiveness until the second coming of Christ
A-millennial	Believes the 1,000-year reign is not literal, but symbolizes Christ reigning in the hearts of believers

Regarding the duration of the white throne of judgment, Scripture does not specify. Yet Revelation 22:3–5 clearly states that the bondservants of Christ will both serve Him and reign with Him in the new heaven and earth forever and ever; therefore, we choose to make **forever** our one-word summary for this section.

THE SEVEN PROPHECIES OF THE CHURCH'S TRIUMPHANT PERIOD

PROPHECY	DURATION
The rapture of the Church	Twinkling of an eye
The great tribulation	7 years?
The second coming of Christ	Not long
The defeat of three enemies	Not long
The millennium	1,000 years
The great white throne of judgment	Not long
The new heaven and new earth	Forever

We do not know when God will fulfill the prophecies of the Triumphant Period of the Church. In fact, Jesus says in Matthew 24:36, "But of that day and hour no one knows, not even the angels of heaven, nor the Son, but the Father alone." He goes on to say in verses 42 and 44, "Therefore be on the alert, for you do not know which day your Lord is coming. . . . For this reason you be ready too; for the Son of Man is coming at an hour when you do not think He will." The apostle John prayed in Revelation 22:20, "Come, Lord Jesus." When the Lord Jesus Christ does return, He will truly astound us. May we stand at the ready.

In the next section we discover the consummation of the theme of Scripture.

WHY?

As we have stressed throughout our attempts to put together the puzzle of the New Testament, the theme of Scripture involves **God receiving glory by restoring fellowship between the nations and Himself through His Son, Jesus Christ.** As we worked our way through the first seven historical periods of the New Testament, we watched as this grand story gathered momentum.

We found that, during the Coming of Christ Era, various individuals and small groups of people respond to the message of God's love and forgiveness. By the middle of the Going of the Church Era, the Good News of Christ penetrates deeper and deeper into the world's various people groups, or what the Scripture calls nations. Now we find that, in the Triumphant Period of the Church, multitudes will surround the throne of God, giving Him glory for reconciling them to Himself. Several passages in the book of Revelation detail this awesome scene.

We find the first passage in Revelation 5. In this chapter, the Lamb of God, the Lord Jesus Christ, prepares to open the book with seven seals, which will begin the judgments of the great tribulation. As He does so, celestial beings give glory to God for redeeming humanity from every tribe, tongue, people group, and nation through the shedding of His blood (Revelation 5:9). Humans, joining heavenly beings in a majestic chorus of praise, declare, "To Him who sits on the throne, and to the Lamb, be blessing and honor and glory and dominion forever and ever" (Revelation 5:13).

A magnificent worship scene, noted two chapters later in Revelation 7, falls between the breaking of the sixth and seventh seals of the book of judgments. We find in verses 9 and 10 "a great multitude, which no one could count, from every nation and all tribes and peoples and tongues, standing before the throne and before the Lamb, clothed in white robes, and palm branches were in their hands; and they cry out with a loud voice, saying, 'Salvation to our God who sits on the throne, and to the Lamb.'" Just imagine! We will belong to that great multitude one day as part of those who by faith in Christ have received salvation from God.

Revelation 15:4, a verse that occurs between the judgments of the trumpets and the bowls, also speaks of all the nations coming and worshiping before God.

CLIMAX OF THE THEME OF THE BIBLE

PASSAGE	EVERY NATION	GIVING GLORY TO GOD
Revelation 5:9–13	"Every tribe and tongue and people and nation"	"Saying, 'To Him who sits on the throne, . . . Blessing and honor and glory and dominion forever and ever'"
Revelation 7:9–10	"A great multitude, . . . from every nation and all tribes and peoples and tongues"	"Saying, 'Salvation to our God'"
Revelation 15:4	"All the nations"	"Worship before [God]"

What a glorious climax to the theme of the Bible, which began in the garden of Eden when Adam and Eve broke fellowship with God through their disobedience. Truly, God deserves to receive all glory and honor and praise for restoring fellowship between the nations and Himself through His Son, the promised Messiah, Jesus Christ the Lord.

We now look at our final author of New Testament Scripture. Let's see what we can learn about his life and writings.

WHO?

To the four Gospel writers (Matthew, Mark, Luke, and John) and the two pillars of the Church (Peter and Paul), we now add the second of

Jesus' half-brothers. Having discussed James, another half-brother, in the previous chapter, we now devote our attention to Jude.

Few people know much about this biblical author because the New Testament rarely mentions him. From Matthew 13:55 and Mark 6:3 we see Jude as one of four half-brothers of Jesus, probably younger than his brother James because of the order of their names. In the original language of the Bible, Jude was referred to as Judas; but English translators began referring to him as Jude. Perhaps they used the abbreviated version of his name so others would not confuse him with Judas Iscariot.

We also know from John 7:3–5 that Jude does not esteem his half-brother as the Messiah at first. Only after the resurrection (Acts 1:14; Jude 1) do we find Jude or any of the half-brothers of Jesus following Him as their Lord and Savior. One other scriptural reference might give some insight into the life of Jude. According to 1 Corinthians 9:5, Jude may have had a wife who accompanied him during his ministry.

Both James and Jude write only one book of the Bible. Each book bears the name of its respective author. The book of Jude contains one characteristic unique among the New Testament books: verses 14 and 15 quote from the book of Enoch, which is extrabiblical Jewish literature.

THE WRITINGS OF JUDE

Jude

Like the second epistle of Peter, Jude's epistle focuses on false teachers. Though the book of Jude consists of only twenty-five verses, it has much to say about our walks with God today. So what can we learn from Jude and his brief address on false teachers? To answer this question, let's first gain a quick overview of his writing.

In the first two verses of his letter, Jude introduces himself and pens a prayer for his readers. In the next two verses he expresses the purpose of his epistle, noting that certain persons have crept into the Church unnoticed. These ungodly people not only teach that it is acceptable to sin but they also deny Jesus as Master and Lord. Concerned about these ungodly people, Jude exhorts his readers to "contend earnestly for the faith."

Jude devotes the bulk of the epistle, verses 5–16, to describing false teachers. In verses 5–7 he shows how God judged people in the past who turned away from the truth: the Hebrews in the wilderness, the angels who left heaven, and the people living in Sodom and Gomorrah. Then in verses 8–16 he switches to present tense and describes the characteristics of "these men." Jude portrays them as defiling the flesh, rejecting authority, reviling angelic majesties, reviling the things they do not understand, grumbling, finding fault, following after their own lusts, speaking arrogantly, and flattering people for the sake of gaining an advantage.

Verses 17–23 provide practical steps on how to "contend earnestly for the faith." He implores his readers to remember that the apostles warned that mockers would arise, to build themselves up in their faith, to pray, to keep themselves in the love of God, to wait anxiously for the mercy of Christ to eternal life, and to help others avoid going astray.

OUTLINE OF THE BOOK OF JUDE

PASSAGE	TOPIC
Verses 1–2	Salutation
Verses 3–4	Concern about false teachers
Verses 5–16	Characteristics of false teachers
Verses 17–23	Cure for false teachers
Verses 24–25	Benediction

Finally, in the last two verses of his book, Jude closes his letter with a beautiful benediction.

FOR NEXT TIME

If you are having an extremely busy week:	If you have a little extra time:	If you can't get enough:
read Hebrews 1–8.	add Hebrews 9–13.	catch up on any reading you have not finished.

PUTTING TOGETHER THE PUZZLE OF THE NEW TESTAMENT

CONCLUSION

CONCLUSION

Admiring the Finished Puzzle

At the beginning of this book, we used the analogy of a thousand-piece puzzle to help us understand how the New Testament fits together. We discovered in the first chapter that the box cover of the puzzle, or rather the theme of the New Testament, displays a picture of **God receiving glory by restoring fellowship between all people groups and Himself through His Son, Jesus Christ the promised Messiah.** We found that the New Testament puzzle has three corner pieces that organize its twenty-seven books: five historical books, twenty-one epistolary books, and one prophetical book.

Chapters two through nine identify and elaborate on the straight-edged pieces of our puzzle. Most of our information came from the five historical books (Matthew, Mark, Luke, John, Acts) plus the one prophetical book (Revelation). The resulting border of the New Testament puzzle consists of two major eras, which we subdivided into eight specific time periods. Within each of these biblical time periods we discovered three to seven key items. Connecting these key items allowed us to chronologically put together the puzzle of the New Testament.

Our diligent persistence to review has finally paid off. We now not only understand the historical flow of the New Testament but we can also communicate it to others. To determine any weak places in our ability to recall what we've learned, let's review one last time the eight New Testament time periods and the corresponding key items by filling in the following charts.

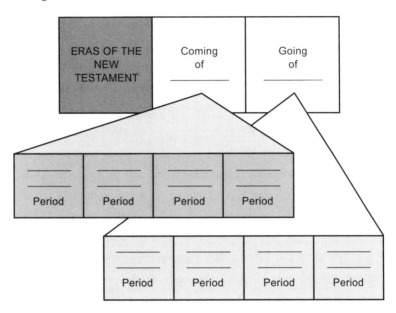

CHRIST'S _____ PERIOD: 7 GROUPS	CHRIST'S _____ PERIOD: 7 THEMES	CHRIST'S _____ PERIOD: 7 DAYS
Born to _____ and _____	Inspires the _____	_____ occurs on Sunday
Worshiped by _____	Instructs the _____	_____ occurs on Monday
Honored by _____ and _____	Infuriates the _____	_____ occurs on Tuesday
Sought by _____ and _____	Causes _____	_____ occurs on Wednesday
Taught by temple _____	Cures the _____	_____ and _____ occur on Thursday
Baptized by _____	Casts out _____	_____ occurs on Friday
Tempted by _____	Reveals that we can be _____	_____ occurs on Saturday

CHRIST'S _____ PERIOD: 3 CONFIDENCE BUILDERS	CHURCH'S _____ PERIOD: 3 EVENTS	CHURCH'S _____ PERIOD: 3 ADVANCES
_____	_____	By _____ to the _____
_____	_____	By _____ to the _____
_____	_____	By _____ to the _____

CHURCH'S _____ PERIOD: 3 IMPRISONMENTS	CHURCH'S _____ PERIOD: 7 PROPHECIES
Paul imprisoned in _____	The _____ of the Church
Paul imprisoned in _____	The great _____
Paul imprisoned in _____	The _____ _____ of Christ
	The defeat of _____ _____
	The _____
	The great _____ _____ of _____
	The new _____ and _____

We devote the rest of this final chapter to strengthening our understanding of the New Testament by consolidating the information gleaned from the previous eight chapters. Staying with our usual approach, we will follow six investigative questions. By doing so, we will reinforce what we've learned as well as gain a few more insights about God's Word.

WHAT?

Let's look first at the *what* question. *What* was God doing in the New Testament? We must view the answer to this question from the perspective of the theme of Scripture. In order for God to restore fellowship between all people groups and Himself, two objectives needed accomplishing.

First, God had to satisfy His law that demanded death as the penalty for mankind's disobedience. He accomplished this objective with the coming of Jesus Christ, the ultimate Passover lamb. This era of the New Testament began with a period of preparation. For approximately the first thirty years of His life, the Lord Jesus simply continued to increase "in wisdom and stature, and in favor with God and men" (Luke 2:52). When ready, He powerfully proclaimed that people can personally experience God's love and forgiveness by believing in Him as the Messiah, the Son of God. At the end of this time of public ministry, He experienced a period of extreme persecution, which culminated with His death on a cross. Despair, however, did not last long. God triumphantly raised His Son from the dead, showing the world that Christ had paid the penalty for humanity's disobedience and that He had provided the way to restored fellowship with God.

Since Christ provided access to God, people needed to know about it. God accomplished this second objective by sending His Church to tell the story of the life, death, burial, and resurrection of Jesus. This era of the New Testament began with the preparation of the Church. Once He had empowered the believers in Christ, He mobilized them to proclaim to the whole world the Good News of eternal life found in a relationship with God through faith in Jesus Christ. Though the Church suffered severe persecution, the story ends with a glorious hope. The final book of the Bible reveals that one day the followers of Christ will all live with God forever in a new heaven and new earth.

ERA	PERIOD	EMPHASIS	SCRIPTURE
Coming of Christ	Private	Preparation of the Messiah	Matt. 1:1–4:11; Mark 1:1–13; Luke 1:1–4:13; John 1:1–18
	Public	Proclamation of the Messiah	Matt. 4:12–20:34; Mark 1:14–10:52; Luke 4:14–19:27; John 1:19–12:11
	Trials	Persecution of the Messiah	Matt. 21:1–27:66; Mark 11:1–15:47; Luke 19:28–23:56; John 12:12–19:42
	Triumphant	Presentation of the Messiah	Matt. 28:1–20; Mark 16:1–20; Luke 24:1–53; John 20:1–21:25
Going of Church	Private	Preparation of the Church	Acts 1:12–2:4
	Public	Proclamation of the Church	Acts 2:5–21:26
	Trials	Persecution of the Church	Acts 21:27–28:31
	Triumphant	Presentation of the Church	Rev. 4–22

The chart above summarizes these two eras with their corresponding eight periods. The third column shows what God emphasized during each time period, while the fourth column identifies where each historical period is recorded in Scripture. This last column proves particularly helpful for the time periods pertaining to the Coming of Christ Era, because the information on the life and ministry of the Lord Jesus comes from the vantage point of four authors.

HOW?

Let's now consider the specifics of how God restored fellowship between Himself and the nations. We'll look at the key items found in each of the historical time periods for both the Coming of Christ Era and the Going of the Church Era. Putting the forty key items together thoroughly tells the story of the New Testament. We've emphasized the forty key items below in boldface italics in order to more easily recognize them.

The New Testament story begins with the Private Period of Christ. Seven groups of people summarize the events of this time. God uses ***Mary and Joseph*** to serve as the earthly parents of Jesus. On the night of the Messiah's birth, ***shepherds*** arrive to worship Him. Approximately six weeks after the Lord's birth in Bethlehem, the family travels to the temple in Jerusalem where ***Simeon and Anna*** honor Him as a light to the Gentiles. After the family returns home to Nazareth, the ***magi and Herod*** seek the Lord but for different reasons. The Gentile magi seek to worship Him, but Herod seeks to slay Him. The Scriptures tell of Jesus at age twelve in Jerusalem, where He is taught by ***teachers*** in the temple. Almost two decades later ***John the Baptist*** baptizes Jesus. After His baptism, Jesus spends forty days fasting in the wilderness, where the ***devil*** tempts Him to disobey God the Father.

Returning from the wilderness experience, Jesus begins His three and a half years of ministry on earth. This Public Period consists of seven themes. The Lord ***inspires the multitudes*** by teaching with great authority the truths of Scripture. While alone with His primary followers He ***instructs the twelve*** disciples. His message often ***infuriates the Pharisees***. The Lord's works give His words credibility. He ***causes miracles*** when He calms a storm and multiplies bread and fish. He reinforces His divinity by ***curing the sick***. Finally, He rampages evil by ***casting out demons.*** The overarching thrust of both Christ's words and works **reveals God's love and forgiveness** that we can receive by faith.

The Coming of Christ Era continues with His Trials Period, summarized by the events that take place over the last seven days of His earthly ministry. On Sunday, as His followers sing of their worship, the Lord marches into Jerusalem in what we know as the **triumphal entry**. The next day Jesus **cleanses the temple** as He declares that the temple should exist as a house of prayer for all nations and not as a robbers' den. On Tuesday, His enemies try to trap Him in a series of questions, while His followers ask about the signs pointing to the end of the age. This time of **questions and answers** proves the occasion of one of Christ's most famous utterances: to love God with all of our heart, soul, mind, and strength. On Wednesday, **Judas plots to betray** Jesus. On Thursday, Jesus spends time with His closest disciples at both **the Last Supper and the garden of Gethsemane**. By Friday morning, after three religious trials and three civil trials, the Romans at the instigation of the Jewish leaders **crucify and bury** Jesus. On Saturday, the seventh in this series of memorable days, **soldiers guard the tomb**.

The Triumphant Period of Christ closes the Coming of Christ Era with three confidence builders for our faith. The period starts with the **empty tomb** of the Lord Jesus Christ. Evidence that God raised Christ from the dead, as opposed to someone stealing the body, comes from the **ten appearances** of the risen Lord recorded in Scripture. These appearances continue for forty days, ending with the **ascension** of Jesus into heaven.

The New Testament's story continues with four historical periods that compose the Going of the Church Era. The Private Period of the Church consists of three events. After the Lord Jesus ascends into heaven at the beginning of the book of Acts, the disciples **return to pray** as they wait for the promise of the Father. During their ten-day wait, Peter guides 120 followers gathered in the upper room as they *replace Judas* with Matthias. On the Day of Pentecost the believers *receive the Holy Spirit*.

Immediately upon receiving the Holy Spirit's filling, the Church enters its Public Period by taking the Good News of the resurrection of Christ to all the nations. The gospel spreads through three advances, each penetrating a different ethnic group and each led by a different leader. The message of Christ goes *to the Jews through Peter* as he preaches four powerful messages in Jerusalem. Persecution in Jerusalem allows communication of the resurrected Jesus *to the Samaritans through Philip* and his bold proclamation of Christ in Samaria. In a series of three missionary journeys, the truth of God's love and forgiveness advances *to the Gentiles through Paul* as he travels across modern-day Turkey and Greece.

By the end of the book of Acts, the Church experiences severe persecution as it enters the Trials Period. Three imprisonments of Paul describe what happens during this time frame. First, the Jews arrest Paul in Jerusalem, resulting in at least two years of incarceration in a *Caesarean jail*. Following a dangerous voyage by ship, Paul arrives in Rome after he appeals to Caesar for a verdict on his case. In the Imperial City he spends at least two years under *Roman house arrest*. Apparently, the emperor declares him innocent, but after a few years of freedom, Paul once again ends up in custody. This time he spends his last days in a *Roman dungeon* before his decapitation.

Though first-century biblical history ends with the Church suffering persecution, it does not leave us with a hopeless future. The books of 1 Thessalonians and Revelation as well as small parts of other books paint a glorious future in what we call the Triumphant Period of the Church. Seven prophecies capture the events that lie ahead for the followers of Christ. The first prophecy informs us that one day Christ will *rapture* His Church. Following (or coinciding with) this amazing event, the Bible prophesies a *great tribulation* lasting for what seems to be seven years. Thousands of years after His ascension, Christ returns. This *second coming of Christ* centers in Jerusalem. Upon His return the Lord Jesus *defeats three enemies*, commonly called the Antichrist, the false prophet, and the devil. With the defeat of this evil triad, Christ reigns peacefully on earth with His followers for one thousand years, which people refer to as *the millennium*. At the end of this thousand years of peace, Christ judges all the wicked who have ever lived and, after pronouncing His verdict, throws them into a lake of fire. The book of Revelation calls this future event *the great white throne of judgment*. The last prophecy calls for the creation of *a new heaven and a new earth* where representatives from every tribe, tongue, and nation live in fellowship with God for eternity, fulfilling and completing the wonderful theme of both the Old and the New Testament.

WHERE?

In the eight periods of the New Testament, we located where each of the events primarily occur. In this section we put them together in order to better understand the general flow of activity throughout the Bible. The numbers on each map below relate to the events detailed on the corresponding chart. From the chart you can then identify what happens at that particular location, where it occurs, and in which historical period it takes place.

Let's begin with the location of the events that occur during the Coming of Christ Era.

Coming of Christ Era

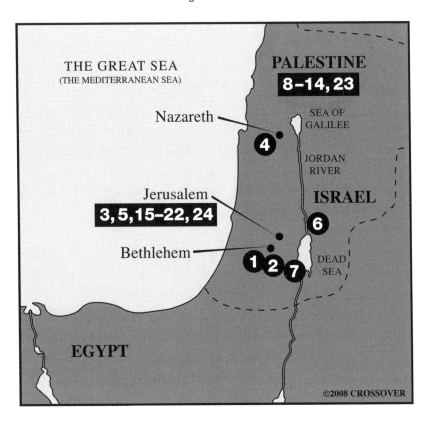

COMING OF CHRIST ERA

NUMBER	WHAT	WHERE	WHEN
1	Born to Mary and Joseph	Bethlehem	Private Period of Christ
2	Worshiped by angels	Bethlehem	Private Period of Christ
3	Honored by Simeon and Anna	Jerusalem	Private Period of Christ
4	Sought by the magi and Herod	Nazareth	Private Period of Christ
5	Taught by temple teachers	Jerusalem	Private Period of Christ

6	Baptized by John the Baptist	Jordan River	Private Period of Christ
7	Tempted by the devil	Wilderness	Private Period of Christ
8	Inspires the multitudes	Throughout Palestine	Public Period of Christ
9	Instructs the disciples	Throughout Palestine	Public Period of Christ
10	Infuriates the Pharisees	Throughout Palestine	Public Period of Christ
11	Causes miracles	Throughout Palestine	Public Period of Christ
12	Cures the sick	Throughout Palestine	Public Period of Christ
13	Casts out demons	Throughout Palestine	Public Period of Christ
14	Reveals that we can be made right with God	Throughout Palestine	Public Period of Christ
15	Triumphal entry	Jerusalem	Trials Period of Christ
16	Cleansing of temple	Jerusalem	Trials Period of Christ
17	Questions and answers	Jerusalem	Trials Period of Christ
18	Judas's plot	Jerusalem	Trials Period of Christ
19	Last Supper and Gethsemane	Jerusalem	Trials Period of Christ
20	Crucifixion	Jerusalem	Trials Period of Christ
21	Guards placed at tomb	Jerusalem	Trials Period of Christ
22	Resurrection	Jerusalem	Triumphant Period of Christ
23	Appearances	Throughout Palestine	Triumphant Period of Christ
24	Ascension	Jerusalem at the Mount of Olives	Triumphant Period of Christ

The next map and chart pertain to the Going of the Church Era. Again, the numbers on the map correspond to the numbers on the chart.

GOING OF THE CHURCH ERA

NUMBER	WHAT	WHERE	WHEN
1	Return to pray	Jerusalem	Private Period of Church
2	Replace Judas	Jerusalem	Private Period of Church
3	Receive the Holy Spirit	Jerusalem	Private Period of Church
4	Gospel to the Jews	Jerusalem	Public Period of Christ
5	Gospel to the Samaritans	Samaria	Public Period of Christ
6	Gospel to the ends of the earth	Roman Empire	Public Period of Christ
7	Caesarean imprisonment	Caesarea	Trials Period of Christ
8	Roman house arrest	Rome	Trials Period of Christ
9	Roman dungeon	Rome	Trials Period of Christ
10	The rapture of the Church	In the clouds	Triumphant Period of Christ
11	The great tribulation	Earth	Triumphant Period of Christ
12	The second coming of Christ	Jerusalem at the Mount of Olives	Triumphant Period of Christ
13	The defeat of three enemies	Lake of fire and the abyss	Triumphant Period of Christ
14	The millennium	Earth	Triumphant Period of Christ
15	The great white throne of judgment	?	Triumphant Period of Christ
16	Eternity fellowshipping with God	New heaven and new earth	Triumphant Period of Christ

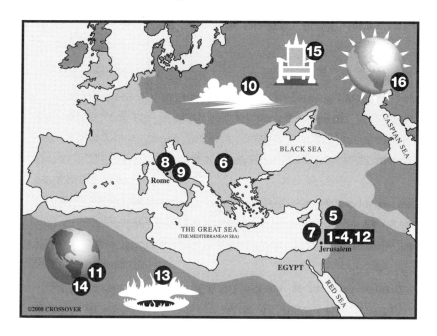

Now let's consider when each of these events occur.

WHEN?

Though we may appreciate knowing when in history various New Testament events occur, it often proves difficult to recall specific dates—except for the year the crucifixion of Christ takes place, and even that historic date may challenge us on bad days. With that realization, the following chart summarizes the dates of important events in the eight New Testament time periods. Note that we've included a few other events in addition to our forty key items. You'll find the additional events in parentheses. Also, recall that Passover and Pentecost occur around April and May, respectively.

	PERIOD	KEY ITEM	APPROXIMATE DATE
COMING OF CHRIST	Private Period	Born to Mary and Joseph	6–4 BC
		Worshiped by shepherds	6–4 BC
		Honored by Simeon and Anna	6–4 BC
		Sought by the magi and Herod	6–4 BC
		Taught by temple teachers	AD 6–8
		Baptized by John the Baptist	AD 26–27
		Tempted by the devil	AD 26–27
	Public Period	Inspires the multitudes	AD 26/27–30
		Instructs the disciples	AD 26/27–30
		Infuriates the Pharisees	AD 26/27–30
		Causes miracles	AD 26/27–30
		Cures the sick	AD 26/27–30
		Casts out demons	AD 26/27–30
		Reveals that we can be made right with God	AD 26/27–30
	Trials Period	Sunday's triumphal entry	AD 30 Passover Week
		Monday's cleansing of temple	AD 30 Passover Week
		Tuesday's questions and answers	AD 30 Passover Week
		Wednesday's Judas's plot	AD 30 Passover Week
		Thursday's Last Supper and Gethsemane	AD 30 Passover Week
		Friday's crucifixion	AD 30 Passover Week
		Saturday's guards placed at tomb	AD 30 Passover Week
	Triumphant Period	Resurrection and empty tomb	AD 30 Sunday after Passover
		Appearances	AD 30 for forty days
		Ascension	AD 30 on fortieth day
GOING OF THE CHURCH	Private Period	Disciples return to pray	AD 30 on fortieth day
		Disciples replace Judas	AD 30 between ascension and Pentecost
		Disciples receive the Holy Spirit	AD 30 on the day of Pentecost

Public Period	Advance of the gospel to Jews	AD 30	
	Advance of the gospel to Samaritans	AD 31	
	(Conversion of Paul)	AD 32	
	Advance of the gospel to Gentiles by Peter	≈ AD 37–38	
	(Herod Agrippa dies)	AD 44	
	Advance of the gospel to Gentiles, Paul's first trip	AD 46–48	
	(Jerusalem Council)	AD 49	
	Advance of the gospel to Gentiles, Paul's second trip	AD 50–52	
	Advance of the gospel to Gentiles, Paul's third trip	AD 53–57	
Trials Period	Arrest and Caesarean imprisonment	≈ May AD 57 to late summer AD 59	
	(Paul's voyage to Rome)	Late summer AD 59 to late winter AD 60	
	Paul's Roman house arrest	Winter AD 60 to spring AD 62	
	(Paul continues his ministry, e.g. Titus 1:5)	AD 62–67	
	Paul's Roman dungeon imprisonment	AD 67	
(Present Times)			
Triumphant Period	The rapture of the Church	Sometime in the future	
	The great tribulation	For seven years after the rapture	
	The second coming of Christ	At the end of the tribulation	
	Defeat of the three enemies	At the second coming of Christ	
	The millennium	For 1,000 years after the second coming of Christ	
	The great white throne of judgment	At the end of the millennium	
	New heaven and new earth	Eternity	

Please remember that unless Scripture or recognized historical events that parallel God's Word give clear indication of the dating of a certain event, we can only approximate the occasion of the above key items. Given that, the above chronology does help us understand when the events of the New Testament occur.

WHY?

In every chapter, we've stressed that the theme of the New Testament as well as the Old Testament displays a picture of **God receiving glory by restoring fellowship between all people groups and Himself through His Son, Jesus Christ the promised Messiah**.

The focus of the Bible centers not on you, me, or any other person. The theme of Scripture focuses on God and God only. Because of who He is and what He has done, only God is worthy to receive glory.

The writers of Scripture stress over and over the glory of God. Matthew, as he quotes the Lord's Prayer, emphasizes, "Our Father who is in heaven, . . . For Yours is the kingdom, and the power, and the glory" (Matthew 6:9, 13). Mark writes of Jesus coming in the glory of His Father (Mark 8:38). Luke tells of the multitude of angels giving glory to God in the highest at the announcement of Christ's birth to the shepherds (Luke 2:14). John reminds his readers of Isaiah seeing God's glory (John 12:41). Peter speaks of God being glorified in all things through Jesus Christ (1 Peter 4:11). In Philippians, Paul confidently asserts that one day every tongue shall confess that Jesus Christ is Lord to the glory of God the Father (Philippians 2:11). James describes Jesus as glorious (James 2:1). Jude in his powerful benediction twice mentions God's glory: "Now to Him who is able to keep you from stumbling, and to make you stand in the presence of His glory blameless with great joy, to the only God our

Savior, through Jesus Christ our Lord, be glory, majesty, dominion and authority, before all time and now and forever. Amen" (Jude 24–25).

But how can we better understand the awesomeness of God's glory? If you recall from our investigation of Matthew in the chapter on the Private Period of Christ, the word *worship* originally came from the Persian language and means "to fall down before a superior and throw kisses in his direction." Keep that image in mind as we see what awaits us one day in heaven. Five times in the book of Revelation John describes the twenty-four elders of heaven falling down and praising the glory of both God the Father and God the Son. Note the emphasized phrases in the following verses.

- "And when the living creatures give *glory* and honor and thanks to Him who sits on the throne, to Him who lives forever and ever, the twenty-four elders will *fall down* before Him who sits on the throne, and will *worship* Him who lives forever and ever, and will cast their crowns before the throne, saying, 'Worthy are You, our Lord and our God, to receive *glory* and honor and power'" (Revelation 4:9–11).

- "When He had taken the book, the four living creatures and the twenty-four elders *fell down* before the Lamb, . . . And they sang a new song, saying, '*Worthy* are You'" (Revelation 5:8–9).

- "And every created thing which is in heaven and on the earth and under the earth and on the sea, and all things in them, I heard saying, 'To Him who sits on the throne, and to the Lamb, be blessing and honor and *glory* and dominion forever and ever.' And the four living creatures kept saying, 'Amen.' And the elders *fell down* and *worshiped*" (Revelation 5:13–14).

- "And the twenty-four elders, who sit on their thrones before God, *fell on their faces* and *worshiped* God, saying, 'We give

Thee thanks, O Lord God, the Almighty, who are and who were, because You have taken Your great power and have begun to reign'" (Revelation 11:16–17).

- "And the twenty-four elders and the four living creatures *fell down* and *worshiped* God who sits on the throne saying, 'Amen. Hallelujah!'" (Revelation 19:4).

Scripture does not reveal the identity of these twenty-four elders, but they must have an extremely exalted position in heaven. Not only does John describe them as elders but also he notes in Revelation 11:16 that they, like God Himself, sit on thrones. Yet even the highest-ranking residents of heaven unashamedly fall on their faces and cast their crowns before God in order to worship and ascribe Him glory.

Pause for a moment and consider these scenes. If the potentates of heaven fall on their faces in recognition of God's superiority, what will we do when we get to heaven to worship our glorious God?

Perhaps we should answer a more practical question. What can we do here on earth for God to receive the glory He deserves? First, give Him glory yourself as you personally take the time to worship Him, not just during corporate and personal times of worship, but throughout the day when your thoughts turn toward Him. Second, gather more worshipers for Him from among the nations, beginning right where you live, in your own Jerusalem. Giving your energies to these two endeavors—being a worshiper and gathering other worshipers—will result in **God receiving glory for restoring fellowship between all people groups and Himself through His Son, Jesus Christ the promised Messiah.** "To Him be the glory forever" (Romans 11:36).

WHO?

Of the many characters found in the New Testament, we chose to focus on the eight people who contributed to the writing of the New Testament: the four Gospel authors, the two pillars of the Church, and the two half-brothers of Jesus. The following chart reminds us of their names and which books of the Bible they wrote.

NEW TESTAMENT AUTHOR	BIBLE BOOKS WRITTEN
Matthew	Matthew
Mark	Mark
Luke	Luke, Acts
John	John; 1, 2 , 3 John; Revelation
Peter	1 and 2 Peter
Paul	Romans, 1 and 2 Corinthians, Galatians, Ephesians, Philippians, Colossians, 1 and 2 Thessalonians, 1 and 2 Timothy, Titus, Philemon, Hebrews (?)
James	James
Jude	Jude

If you visit the website at www.ciu.edu/NTBibleStudy and scroll down to "Publications," you'll find a Bible study from each New Testament author that will help transform your walk with God. In many ways, what you learn from the website may prove far more important than the information in this book. Why? Because we can know every event in the life of Christ, recite hundreds of memory verses, and communicate with confidence the events related to the end times from the book of Revelation, but if we do not allow God the Father to continually transform us into the image of His Son through the power of His Spirit, then what we know doesn't matter much.

May the Word of God master us as we seek to master the Word of God.

PUTTING TOGETHER THE PUZZLE

The following chart puts together the puzzle of the New Testament by summarizing all the information covered by our six investigative questions of the eight periods of biblical history of the Coming of Christ Era and the Going of the Church Era. You may want to make a copy of the following pages and place them in the front of your Bible. That way if you need a quick refresher, you will always have immediate access to the information.

PERIOD	CHRIST'S PRIVATE PERIOD	CHRIST'S PUBLIC PERIOD	CHRIST'S TRIALS PERIOD	CHRIST'S TRIUMPHANT PERIOD
SCRIPTURE	Matthew 1; Luke 2; Matthew 2–4	John 1–4; Mark 1–9; John 7–11	Luke 19–23	John 20–21
WHAT?	Preparation of the Messiah	Proclamation of the Messiah	Persecution of the Messiah	Presentation of the Messiah
HOW?	7 Groups • Born to Mary and Joseph • Worshiped by shepherds • Honored by Simeon and Anna • Sought by the magi and Herod • Taught by temple teachers • Baptized by John the Baptist • Tempted by the devil	7 Themes • Words: Inspires the multitude • Words: Instructs the Twelve • Words: Infuriates the Pharisees • Works: Causes miracles • Works: Cures the sick • Works: Casts out demons • Way: Reveals that we can be made right with God	7 Days • Sunday: Triumphal entry • Monday: Cleansing the temple • Tuesday: Questions and answers • Wednesday: Judas's plot • Thursday: Last Supper, Gethsemane, two trials • Friday: Four trials, crucifixion, burial • Saturday: Soldiers placed at tomb	3 Confidence Builders • Empty tomb • Ten appearances • Ascension
WHERE?	Nazareth	Capernaum	Jerusalem	Jerusalem
WHEN?	≈ 30 Years	≈ 3½ Years	One week	40 days
WHY?	So the nations can glorify God	So the nations can glorify God	So the nations can glorify God	So the nations can glorify God
WHO?	Matthew (Matthew)	Mark (Mark)	Luke (Luke, Acts)	John (John, 1–3 John, Revelation)

PERIOD	CHURCH'S PRIVATE PERIOD	CHURCH'S PUBLIC PERIOD	CHURCH'S TRIALS PERIOD		CHURCH'S TRIUMPHANT PERIOD
SCRIPTURE?	Acts 1	Acts 2–21	Acts 22–28		Revelation 4–22
WHAT?	Preparation of the Church	Proclamation of the Church	Persecution of the Church		Presentation of the Church
HOW?	3 Events • Return to pray • Replace Judas • Receive the Holy Spirit	3 Advances • Peter to Jews • Philip to Samaritans • Paul to Gentiles	3 Imprisonments of Paul • Cesarean jail • Roman house arrest • Roman dungeon (Mamertine)	PRESENT TIMES	7 Prophecies • The rapture of the Church • The great tribulation • The second coming of Christ • The defeat of three enemies • The millennium • The great white throne of judgment • The new heaven and new earth
WHERE?	Jerusalem	Antioch	Rome		New heaven and new earth
WHEN?	10 Days	27 Years	10 Years		Eternity
WHY?	So the nations can glorify God	So the nations can glorify God	So the nations can glorify God		So the nations can glorify God
WHO?	Peter (1 and 2 Peter)	Paul (Rom., 1 and 2 Cor., Gal., Eph., Phil., Col., 1 and 2 Thess., 1 and 2 Tim., Titus, Philem.) (Hebrews?)	James (James)		Jude (Jude)

ALSO AVAILABLE

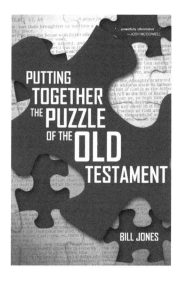

Intimidated! Overwhelmed! Totally confused! Descriptives such as these suggest how we often feel when it comes to the Old Testament. No wonder, with eight to nine hundred pages of names like Melchizedek, Mephibosheth, Meshelemiah, Michmethath, Mikhtam, who wouldn't feel this way?

If the Old Testament were one of those 1,000-piece puzzles, then this book provides the puzzle's box cover so you can understand the complete picture of what you are assembling. It also helps you put together the important four corners and all the straight-edged pieces so you have a completed border or frame of reference for the puzzle. Armed with these two advantages, when you read or study Old Testament stories, you will understand how all the pieces fit together.

This book is ideal for those who have little or no familiarity with the Old Testament or for pastors and lay leaders to help teach a better understanding of the Old Testament.

Retail: $16.99
ISBN: 978-1-93280-594-9

Available for purchase online or through your local bookstore.

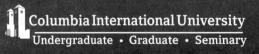